JENN HENRY
Lifestyle Recovery Expert

RESILIENCE
A different kind of strong

Resilience: A Different King of Strong
Copyright © 2023 by Jenn Henry

Printed in the United States of America

Hardcover ISBN: 978-1-960876-14-0
Paperback ISBN: 978-1-960876-15-7
Ebook ISBN: 978-1-960876-16-4
Library of Congress Control Number: 2023941473

Muse Literary
3319 N. Cicero Avenue
Chicago IL 60641-9998

A LOVE LETTER TO MY READER . . .

Dear Reader,

There will be moments, as you are reading through this book, when you feel uncomfortable. Moments that make you question your beliefs and challenge who you are as a person . . .

But stay with me.

Because this book isn't meant to be comfortable, it is meant to change your life.

It's not going to lie to you and tell you it's all magically going to be okay and that this book will fix all of your problems, heal all of your wounds, and make you millions of dollars.

Because it won't.

What it will do is guide you, step-by-step, through creating a life that you look forward to waking up to every single day. A sustainable life and career of serving others while still experiencing a life of true personal freedom.

It will teach you how to take inspired action instead of fear-based action.

It will help you double-down on what is truly important to you and let go of what isn't.

It will make you look at what is and isn't working in your relationships, your health, your career, your finances, and your spirituality.

It will make you decide your own truth and your own path, without the need to people-please or fit into a preconceived notion of what your life is "supposed" to look like.

I wrote this book to help you TAKE YOUR POWER BACK and create an epic life of true personal freedom.

You deserve a life you love.

You deserve happiness, success, health, and abundance.

You deserve this.

Cheers to Living Your Best Life!

XO
Jenn
P.S.
Take care of yourself, my friend.
I promise, you're worth it.

PS.

In order to make sure you are fully supported in your personal journey through this book, I've created a QR code for you to scan that gives you an all access pass to the Resilience Book Portal, where you will find all of the worksheets, journaling prompts, exercises and moments of pause and reflection featured throughout.

This is not just a book. This is an experience and I want you to be able to make the most of it.

See you on the other side!

CONTENTS

PART ONE

CONNECTION

Chapter One

CHRONIC DISCONNECTION

2017

As the heat from the bright lights beat down on me, beads of sweat began to trickle down my back.

My poses were crisp and clean, the result of months of painfully awkward practice, coupled with hours upon hours in the gym and in the kitchen, all leading up to this very moment.

My muscles were starting to cramp, but that was nothing new. I could handle it. I just needed to keep my breaths short and my stomach in.

Don't breathe, Jenn ... don't breathe or it will all fall apart ... you've sacrificed everything for this ... don't fuck it up ...

I was on stage, battling for first place in a fitness competition with a woman at least fifteen years older. Self-doubt and insecurities filled my head, so like all insecure women do, I began picking her apart.

From close range, I could see the flaws behind the façade of health and fitness: the thinning hair, the knots and scars on her hips from years of PED injections, the loose skin hanging slack from her body—the result of being repeatedly filled out and dieted down. I was struck by the irony that this woman was falling apart in her quest to become the picture of health. All for a plastic trophy and the hopes that one day she could be an unpaid professional athlete.

The revelation hit me like a ton of bricks.

Was this my future?

I was walking around at less than 10 percent body fat, hadn't had a period in over three years, and my kidneys were shutting down from too much protein. I was constantly judging myself, pinching my skin to see if I had gained any fat, wearing corsets that made it impossible to breathe so I could create that envied hourglass frame, and I was never *ever* satisfied. I hated who I saw in the mirror, never saw my friends, rarely ever went out to eat, and was now battling it out on stage with someone who, if I was totally honest, I didn't really even want to be compared to.

What in the actual fuck?

What was I doing?

How did I get to this point?

I realized I had completely disconnected from what I *really* wanted.

This wasn't what I had signed up for. This wasn't the experience I'd imagined.

When I first started working out seven years prior, it wasn't to *look* any kind of way. It was to *feel* some kind of way. It was to learn how to cope.

It was to find sanity.

It was to learn how to breathe through fear, pain, and discomfort.

It was to build confidence in myself, to feel comfortable in my own skin, and to find a way to live a balanced, healthy life that I loved. It was a chance to truly experience freedom from the unruly thoughts and emotions I'd been plagued by my entire life.

It was not *this*.

Almost a decade prior to this, in October of 2010, I was released from The California Institute for Women State Correctional Facility (CIW) and escorted directly to a six-month inpatient women's treatment program called New Hope in Beaumont, California.

Up until this time, like so many others today, I suffered from what I like to call Chronic Disconnection: the need to "fix" my current reality by escaping into something else.

We all have our favorite fix, whether it's Netflix, food, sex, shopping, other people's drama, or the widely recognized favorite duo—alcohol and drugs.

Growing up, I had no emotional regulation (manic depressive/ bipolar), was extremely empathetic (cared way too much), and took on the world as if it was my job to make everyone okay (codependent only child).

As an only child, I found myself constantly seeking connection with others. I didn't have any brothers or sisters and always felt like something was missing.

I spent my entire childhood as a chameleon. Whatever you liked, I liked. I was whoever you needed me to be so that you'd like and accept me. I didn't know who I was or how to be okay in my own skin. I would constantly compare myself to the other kids and always felt so different and out of place.

I was diagnosed with bipolar-manic depression at the age of thirteen. I didn't know what that meant, but they told me it was because I had difficulty regulating my emotions.

Duh.

I didn't need a doctor to tell me that. Or that I lacked the ability to focus for long periods of time or that too much went on in my head at once or that my constant impatience stemmed from the fact that I was, shall we say, too smart for my own good.

My brain just worked differently than other kids'.

While I am grateful for that now, I definitely wasn't then. I just never really felt like I fit.

So, to make this square peg fit into the round hole they had designated for me, they started me on psych meds. Anything to make me the good little girl they wanted me to be.

People-pleasing quite literally almost killed me.

Here I was again, on a damn *stage*, trying to look like someone or be something I wasn't, just for some sense of validation that I was good enough.

Even worse, I was losing any sense of myself all over again in the process.

I realized on that stage, right then and there, I needed to make a shift. I didn't know what I wanted, but I knew what I didn't and that was enough. This wasn't the first time in my life that I knew I needed to make a change.

Somehow, I needed to become a different kind of strong.

Pause and Reflect

Take a moment to reflect on where you are in your life at the moment.

If there was anything you could change, what would that be?

What just isn't working anymore?
What would you want instead?

February 2009

The pain actually woke me up.

Every nerve ending in my body was on fire.

My pulse ached in my bones as I cried out for help.

I needed the pain to stop.

I just needed it to go away, just for a minute.

Just a moment of relief . . .

But no one was there.

Then I remembered where I was.

I had been arrested the week prior for drug possession and stolen property, violating the terms of my parole and sending me back to county jail to face six years and my second term in prison.

The ironic part is, I literally went down for other people both times I did hard time.

The rule was simple: You don't tell or you are a rat or a snitch, and that is one of the most *dangerous* labels to be tagged with on the streets *or* in prison.

As someone who was already a codependent people-pleaser, God knows there was no way I'd rat on anyone. So, I did time for crimes other people actually committed because the hotel room the police raided was in my name or the car they used to commit crimes was registered to me.

I know, smart, right?

Don't get me wrong, I absolutely deserved to get arrested and serve time, and to be clear, getting arrested saved my life. I was killing myself—buying, using, and selling drugs, robbing people, stealing, committing fraud, and absolutely living a criminal life. I am eternally grateful for the laws that were in place during my years on the streets because I wouldn't be here to tell you this story of redemption if they hadn't stepped in and saved me from myself.

But at the time, it felt like my world was on fire.

Because it was.

When they raided my hotel room during this last arrest, I had been on a sixty-seven-day meth run since my release from my *first* prison term just a few months before. As I sat there quietly on the curb while the Riverside Police Department was preoccupied searching my hotel room and questioning the other suspects, I carefully tucked the drugs and needle I had stashed on me "away" for my trip to county jail.

If you are wondering how, think *tampon*.

It was different getting arrested this time. I'd lost count of how many times I'd been picked up by the cops. Too many apparently, because they even knew me by name now.

"What's up, Henry? Haven't seen you around in a while . . . you just get out?" they asked, knowing full well I had because they were the ones who had arrested me the year prior.

"Yeah, says here she's only been out sixty-seven days now."

"Congratulations, Ms. Henry! You've just scored yourself a parole violation and another vacation."

They patted me down, read me my rights, handcuffed me, put me in the back of the cop car, and drove me to the station for booking.

During processing, I wasn't even phased. It had become almost routine: the fingerprinting, photos, stripping down nude to cough and squat in front of the officers. I was laughing and chatting with the cops like it was just another day. The fact was, I knew that I was set. I knew that the drugs I was sneaking in to sell gave me power. I had the control. This wasn't my first rodeo. Now I knew how to play the game, and I planned on winning.

The first week or so went just as I had planned. My bunkie (cellmate) helped me to trade half of the drugs I had for all of the toiletries, snacks, and supplies I could fit in my 18 in. x18 in. cubby. We would stay up and get high together, and since she had been there for a little while already, fighting her case, she was able to introduce me to who I needed to know in order to get what I wanted.

It was perfect . . .

Until the drugs ran out, of course.

My bunkie was six feet, two inches tall, 250 pounds, had a shaved head, and the kind of presence that made you question your every move. I mean, they literally called her "Six-Two."

When I was coming down, or burning out after a long run on meth, I wasn't exactly the most tolerant or rational human being. I was bitter and angry and blamed anyone and everyone else for where I'd ended up.

One evening, I snapped. I honestly can't even remember what she said to me, but apparently I didn't like it. Of course, since I was detoxing from an assortment of recreational drugs, I didn't care who she was, how big she was, or how intimidated I actually might have been if I had been in my right mind. I attacked her head-on. Without even skipping a beat, she blocked my advances, picked me up like a rag doll, and threw me across the cell. Then, of all things, she picked up a Bible, chucked it at my head, and spat at me.

"You need God, bitch!"

Then she simply climbed into her bunk, rolled over, and went to sleep.

Probably not the most spiritual introduction to the Word of God, but there it was.

I stood up, seething now more than ever, angrily tossed the Bible up into my cubby, climbed up into my bunk, and passed out for the next few days.

When I woke up, I looked out to the day room through the small, skinny window slit in the center of our solid steel cell door. Six-Two was in the day room playing cards and laughing with the other girls. I looked around at the different cliques of women, calling their families, writing to their friends and loved ones, playing games. Somehow, they all seemed okay. They all seemed like they were holding it together and dealing with everything just fine. Meanwhile, I felt more alone than ever. I had single-handedly destroyed every relationship in my life: my parents, friends, family—shoot, not even my dealer from the neighborhood wanted anything to do with me anymore.

I was crazy.

I was a lost cause.

I was too far gone.

Now my bunkie didn't like me, either. The drugs were what had kept us cordial, and once they ran out, we were no longer playing nice. Neither one of us wanted to be here and now, our escape was gone. Years of numbed emotions and experiences were all bubbling to the surface, and it was more than I could bear.

I needed relief only the numbness of drugs could give me, so I scrambled weakly out of my bunk to my hiding spot and grabbed the old, used syringe I'd stashed away. I climbed back up and huddled under my blankets. I repeatedly poked my ankles over and over again, trying to register in any vein I could find, so that I could extract any residue that might have been left behind in the barrel.

Anything to escape this . . .

Blood speckled the sheets as my hands shook and my heart raced with the anticipation of the escape . . . for that freeing moment of relief.

But then something else happened.

I found myself having an out-of-body experience on the other side of the room.

I was taken aback at what I saw.

The girl I was staring at was me, but it wasn't. She was so thin you could see every bone in her face. Her jail scrubs hung off her body like a child wearing her father's work coveralls. Her hair was thin and matted, and she was covered in blood streaks and scars.

Was this me?

Was this what I really looked like?

How had I gotten to this point?

A devastating sense of pity and sadness filled my heart as I stared at a girl who was barely existing. She sat there lifeless, lost, and broken, disconnected from any sense of being, longing for something, but not knowing what.

In what seemed like the same moment, I was back in my body. The desperation and pain were almost more than I could bear. I quickly realized that for that small sliver of time, the pain had been gone. The fear and loneliness hadn't existed, and I had felt a relief and a freedom I didn't know was possible.

I looked up to the corner of the cell, to the place I had viewed myself from, and there sat the Bible I had tossed into the cubby a few nights before.

I had never been a religious person. I'm still not but stay with me for a minute.

I uncovered myself and reached for the book. I didn't know where to turn, so I simply opened and started to read.

My eyes were immediately drawn to a verse that changed everything: 1 Peter 1:13.

It told me to "gird up the loins of my mind and be sober" and that I would find grace in the revelation of God.

How had I turned exactly to that page and that verse? How did it speak to me so clearly in that moment?

I somehow just knew that I needed to get right in my mind and body so I could connect with my Spirit—the highest part of myself.

The part of God that was and is inside of me.

Whether you call it "Source" or the "Divine" or "God," there is a part of you that transcends all that is of this world.

There is a source that resides in all of us that is all knowing and this just happened to be where mine was able to break through.

That moment woke up a part of me that I didn't know existed. The part that still actually cared about *me*. *My* well-being. *My* happiness.

I realized, in that moment, that after everything I'd done and all the people that I'd hurt, I still wasn't alone. This divine source would always be there. Even after all I had done to destroy myself, it still cared.

I realized that whether I liked it or not, I was still here and I wasn't going anywhere. Even though I didn't know what it was, I had a purpose. There was a reason I was still here.

There *had* to be.

I don't know if I can truly express the kind of comfort and hope it gave me, knowing that when it came down to it, a part of me knew who I was and what I needed to do.

I just needed to start paying closer attention.

Until then, I had always been my own worst enemy. Growing up, I didn't know how to take care of myself. I wouldn't shower unless I was told to, or even get ready at all. I'd roll out of bed as the car was leaving for school, throw on the same Calvin Kline sweatshirt off the floor that I'd worn the day before, skip breakfast, and when I did finally eat, it was an Abba Zaba and a bag of salsa verde Doritos. I had terrible cystic acne and was mortified by my own reflection, uncomfortable in my own skin and disconnected every chance I got.

I didn't know who I was, so I would pretend to be anything for anyone, even if they were mean to me. I just wanted them to accept me. Yet here I was, in jail, at my lowest point ever, and I was actually concerned about *my own* well-being, maybe for the first time in my entire life.

I was shaken to my core.

It was this exact moment when I realized that I am the only one who can change my circumstances. I am the only one who can determine the direction of my life. I really am the only one who knows what is best for me, but I *have* to start *listening*.

I had already been to prison once ... and was worse when I came out then when I went in. I didn't need to be housed with murderers and thieves. I needed to be taught real life skills I could use in my own recovery. I needed actual treatment.

For months, I fought my case in court. I knew that if I just went back to prison, nothing would change. I needed help. I needed to learn how to cope, how to actually deal with my feelings, and not try to numb everything. I had to learn how to do life on life's terms. I had to learn how to be okay in my own skin and stop questioning everything. I didn't want to just keep disconnecting from life.

In creating a lifestyle of whole-health recovery over the last twelve years, I have realized a few things:

I needed to get connected. Not to others this time but to myself.

I needed to stop judging myself so harshly and build a loving relationship and a conscious connection to my highest, most authentic self.

I needed to stop people-pleasing and figure out what lit *me* up. What gave *me* life. What *I* liked and what *I* didn't.

I needed to stop wandering aimlessly through life and create a vision of what I wanted.

I needed to start getting honest with myself about what I was saying 'yes' to and what I was saying 'no' to, and I had to find a way to hold my highest self accountable.

The Freedom Framework that I have outlined in this book for you has given me the freedom to create a sustainable life and career of serving others, by making my own health and happiness a priority. The Freedom Framework consists of six simple steps:

1. Connection
2. Alignment
3. Balance
4. Boundaries
5. Authenticity
6. Accountability

By working through these steps, I have learned how to create the experiences that I want, instead of being a victim of my circumstances.

I have learned how to create a life of personal and professional freedom while still making an incredible impact in this world.

I have learned how to be okay, even when I am uncomfortable.

If a formerly homeless, IV-drug-addicted convict with severe mental health issues like me can create an amazing life, so can you.

Pause and Reflect

What are the circumstances, labels, thoughts, or beliefs (old stories) that you have convinced yourself will keep you from having the life you want?

Hop into the book portal to learn a way to shift those limiting beliefs into power statements that turn those circumstances into strengths.

I'd love to say it's been a smooth ride ever since my moment of awakening, but of course that would be a flat-out lie.

The truth is, old habits die hard. I had programmed myself to believe certain things for so long that they had become my truth.

I am twelve years into this journey of lifestyle recovery and I still have plenty of moments of disconnection. But now, they are fewer and farther between.

Today, I am more comfortable in my own skin than I ever have been, and it's all because I learned how to consciously connect to my current experience. Once I am connected to my current experience, then, if I want, I can make a shift. When I connect to the fact that I am the only one who can determine my experiences in this life, I can take back my power, shift my experience, and decide to create a new one. If I don't want to experience fear, then I can choose faith. If I don't want to experience longing, then I need to direct my focus to gratitude.

But if I don't connect, I can't identify.

I have learned that for most of us, our anxiety stems from our inability to be present. We are either stuck in the past or worrying about the future.

There is a big difference between worrying about the future and preparing for it.

My goal is to set you up for the latter.

When we connect to the now, we ground ourselves into what is real. We create safety and belonging, which gives us the ability to do the things that we may have hesitated to do out of fear. Whether it's fear of judgment, failure, or of wasting your time, it is stopping you from living the life you want and I want to help remove its power over you.

When we are stuck in the past, our old beliefs have a way of convincing us that what happened before is bound to happen again, no matter how you or your circumstances have changed.

This keeps us from being able to make clear decisions or take inspired action towards our goals.

I invite you to continue to dive deeper into the steps in this book with an open mind, ready to take inspired action. The life you want is on the other side of this work.

Chapter Two

CURRENT LOCATION

Over the years, I have received a ridiculous amount of therapy and have been to countless masterminds, workshops, retreats, and life-coaching events. Every single time, they wanted me to create a vision first.

October 2010

In the beginning of my journey into Lifestyle Recovery, I remember sitting in a group therapy session in the treatment program I was admitted to when I first arrived from prison. New Hope was a state-funded residential drug and alcohol treatment program for women released from prison to help them integrate back into society and reconnect with their children.

The huge, weathered, yellow house sat on the corner of a busy street in a small town called Beaumont, California.

There were sixty women and quite a few of their children living in one house, all struggling to learn how to function in the real world.

Some of us were brand new and would be in group sessions working with counselors from 9:00 a.m.-5:00 p.m. every day.

Those that were farther along in the program were free to go to school or go find jobs, but we all started and ended our day together.

During one of my first weeks in our group sessions, they asked us to tell them where we saw ourselves in ten years. They wanted to know what we wanted for our lives—in detail.

I didn't even know what I wanted for breakfast.

I had been through so much already in my life that my vision was skewed. My perspective was so twisted, I had no way to even imagine what was possible for me, other than the life I was already living.

How could I imagine a life I didn't think I was capable of having? I believed some people were meant to have success and abundance, while others were meant to live in hustle and scarcity.

Growing up, I believed I was destined for abundance. But somewhere along the way, my beliefs shifted.

Living on the streets, being taken advantage of, and treated like trash on the side of the road doesn't really do much for one's ambition or self-esteem. I had been deemed powerless in so many ways; how was I supposed to believe I could really take back my power and create some successful, magnificent life?

Once again, I felt like I didn't fit in the box they were asking me to step into. The strategy that seemed to work for everyone else wasn't working for me. I had no clue what I wanted, but I sure as hell knew what I didn't want. So, maybe I had to go about asking my own questions.

I began to get curious.

I knew I didn't want to feel so out of place all of the time, so maybe that meant I wanted to feel like I was a part of something.

I knew I didn't want to keep numbing and disconnecting from life, so maybe I needed to learn how to be okay with feeling things and being present.

I didn't want to keep pretending I was someone or something I wasn't, so I needed to figure out who I was, what I wanted, and what it really looked like to step into my true authentic self.

I didn't want to keep repeating the same patterns, so I realized I needed some way to hold myself accountable

It was finally making sense. Now I had an idea of what *I* wanted:

To be a part of something bigger than myself

To be okay in my own skin and be present in my current experience

To live an honest, authentic life

Accountability for myself and my circumstances

I noticed it was quiet in the room. I looked around and saw that everyone was looking at me, including the counselor. Apparently she was having to repeat a question to me.

"I'll ask again. Where do you see yourself in ten years, Miss Henry?"

The counselor stood there, curiously gazing over the top of her reading glasses, patiently waiting for me to respond.

I replied hesitantly, "As a part of something much bigger than myself, comfortable in my own skin, living an honest, authentic life, and held fully accountable to the part of God inside myself."

She stood there, mildly impressed and confused at the same time. It was not like any of the answers she had heard before mine:

"Successful with a good job, a nice car, my kids and my family . . ."

"Owning a home . . ."

"Running a business . . .".

I couldn't see any of that and wasn't even sure if I wanted those things. I needed to redefine what *my* definition of success looked like so I could set goals that would support the experiences *I* wanted to have.

I wanted to experience what it was to feel like a part of something. To know who I was. To be okay in the present and become the most authentic version of myself. To do that, I needed to start saying 'no' to what wasn't working and 'yes' to what was. I needed to learn how to hold space for who I was capable of being, without judgment and so much damn self-doubt.

If I didn't, how was I going to be able to make the decisions that were actually best for me?

I had no clue how it was going to happen, but it had to. I couldn't keep going the way I was. I had to figure out how to connect to myself, my feelings and emotions, my thoughts and beliefs, and my current experience.

I could probably write an entire second book based solely on what I learned about myself during my stay at New Hope, but for this story, I will just be giving you the highlights.

I realized that by being so disconnected, I had never had the opportunity to truly experience life.

I was so afraid of feeling too much or being too much that I would just rather not exist.

I didn't want to live, but I was too scared to die, so I was on what we call "suicide on the installment plan," slowly killing myself with my unhealthy habits and destructive lifestyle.

Connection had to come first.

If I didn't learn how to feel, if I didn't learn how to "be" or how to feel comfortable in my own skin, I would never be able to take control of my own life.

But how?

Think of it like Google Maps. In order to get where we are going in the most efficient way, we need step-by-step directions. For accurate directions, we need a current location and a destination. This section is about our current location.

The first step to knowing what to do, or deciding which direction we need to go, is to get clear and connected to our current experience: What are we experiencing in the current moment?

The most important part is to do this without judgment.

It's simply time to get curious.

One way to do this is by checking in on your "Basic Five":

1. Health

2. Relationships

3. Career

4. Finances

5. Spiritual Connection

You can always go deeper. When I work with my clients, we separate their lives into more categories like Physical Health, Mental Health, Emotional Health, Play and Joy, Rest and Recovery, Personal Growth, etc. but for this book, we will keep to the basic five areas I shared.

I invite you to practice the meditation, journaling, breathing, and state-change exercises in this book along with me, or to read through the book and come back to start the exercises from the beginning. Either way, you will find all you need in the book portal. Simply hold your phone camera up to the QR code and click the link that pops up.

It will escort you directly to all of the worksheets, guided meditations, and any exercises I share with you throughout the book.

In order to clearly identify where you are in these different areas, first you will have to get present and connected to your current experience.

This can be difficult to do if you are just beginning, so remember to be patient with yourself. Try different exercises and practices before you throw in the towel. Start with just one and do your best to remain open to what comes up, even if it is uncomfortable. It is in this discomfort we usually find the most clarity.

Easy ways to get connected:

- Breath Work
- Stretching and Yoga
- Grounding
- Meditation
- Journaling

- Tapping - Emotional Brain Training (EBT)
- Exercising
- Gardening
- Mirror Work

This is a huge list. But the thousand-mile journey starts with a single step.

So choose one. I started with breathing, but choose what feels best to you.

Be still and listen.

This is where your truth is.

Pause and Reflect

Once you choose the technique you are most curious about, flip ahead and find the section that describes it in detail.

Take a few moments once you begin to notice what comes up for you in your body. What thoughts start to surface? What feelings?

Reflect on and journal about what comes up for you.

Let go of any judgments or opinions about where you think you "should" be.

Instead, be open, curious, and loving.

Chapter Three

BREATH WORK

Breathing.

Seems super basic, right?

You may be surprised that I am going to focus an entire chapter on breathing. You may be thinking, *Seriously, Jenn? Breathing? I obviously have to breathe or I would die. We all do it naturally.*

But do we? So often, people don't realize that they are holding their breath, taking shallow breaths, or breathing more rapidly than normal.

The first time someone asked me to take a deep breath, I almost laughed at them.

I was sitting in a room with hundreds of other coaches and industry leaders and I felt like an imposter, completely out of place. I had signed up for a training event to take my business to the next level.

Here I was with no degree or any credentials that made me an "expert." I wasn't making six figures a year like everyone else in the room, I didn't have a thriving coaching business yet, I didn't even have a business plan. My anxiety was through the roof, my head was spinning, and I sat there, wringing my hands, at the edge of my seat, waiting for this "expert" to tell me what to do . . . and then it happened. They wanted me to take a deep breath.

That was their answer. Their "cure-all." Their magic potion.

Breathing? Come on, now. I'd paid a few hundred dollars to be in the room taking this training and they wanted me to *breathe?*

Give me a break.

But this dude was serious.

Okay, I'll play, I thought, and I tried to take a deep breath.

Nothing happened.

Not because I didn't try, but because I hadn't realized I had been holding my breath the entire time.

I realized that first, for me to breathe, I had to let go. I had to exhale. I had to create space.

For years, I had been holding my breath without realizing it. I'd probably been doing it my entire life. No wonder I felt like I was suffocating and suffered chronic panic attacks! I wasn't freaking breathing!

For me, it wasn't just about taking a breath, it was about letting it go. It was about allowing the breath to follow its natural course through my body, while breaking the tendency to keep it pent up inside of me.

Did you know that your breathing is what actually regulates your fight, flight, or freeze response?

In science, we call this the sympathetic response.

Some symptoms you may notice are racing thoughts, rapid heartbeat, sweating, emotional imbalance, emotional disconnection, yelling or fighting with someone, hiding under the covers instead of doing all the things on your to-do list, and a myriad of other fun activities to try to keep ourselves safe.

In order to turn that off and turn on the parasympathetic response system (which is our rest and digest setting—yes, breathing actually helps with digestion too) we need to regulate our nervous system by taking long, deep breaths.

If everyone paid attention to how they were breathing, we wouldn't all be so anxious all the time.

A large part of anxiety, if not all, is caused by our inability to be in the present. We are so worried about the past or the future that we start to feel unsafe and either need to fight, flee, or freeze, causing us to hold our breath. This puts us in a constant state of uncertainty regarding our safety and security. Hence the anxiety.

Breathing will be the first step to any meditation, journaling, or grounding exercises, as you need your mind and body to begin to align before anything else.

Let's try it.

Find a focus point or close your eyes.

Take a deep breath, counting to five.

Hold at the top of the breath for the count of five.

Breathe out slowly with control for the count of seven.

Repeat three-five times.

You may notice a strange tingling sensation in your face or fingertips. This is proof your body isn't getting enough oxygen on a daily basis.

When we learn how to breathe, we are learning how to regulate our nervous system, promote relaxation, and lower stress levels. Lowering stress levels is proven to help us live longer, happier lives.

When we can regulate our nervous system, and get ourselves out of the state of fight, flight, or freeze, we will be able to stop subconsciously worrying about keeping ourselves safe and will begin to make thoughtful decisions and take inspired action towards what we are meant to do and who we are meant to be in this life.

It's a win-win.

Chapter Four

STRETCHING AND YOGA

It was actually during my first prison term in the Central California Women's (CCW) facility in Chowchilla that I was initially introduced to yoga.

I had never been to a class before, and it took quite a bit of convincing from one of the lifers to get me to go.

I mean, who does yoga in prison?

Wasn't that for rich housewives with nothing else to do? Or for the peace-loving hippies who don't shave their armpits?

I had no clue what it was all about but after months of her persisting, I caved.

I walked into the room and saw quite a few women who I knew were actually there.

A few I definitely did *not* expect to see. Hardened criminals, thugs, gangsters . . . *doing yoga?*

I chuckled to myself at the revelation.

I guess I could at least give it a chance.

I was instructed to take a seat on one of the yoga mats scattered around on the old indoor-outdoor carpet in the classroom.

Over the course of the hour, the yoga instructor gently and lovingly guided us through specific movements and breathing, quieting our minds, and allowing our bodies to ebb and flow with the rhythm of the music.

For just a few of those moments, I wasn't in prison anymore. It actually didn't matter where I was.

I was at peace.

Looking back, I can see that it really was my first experience connecting with my breath. Connecting with my body. Being present without the anxiety, fear, resentment, and self- loathing. I was stretching myself in uncomfortable ways, but I welcomed the discomfort.

I had beaten my body down for so long, it felt good to be doing something to honor its sacrifice.

The fact is, many of us started developing terrible posture and breathing habits at a pretty young age, no matter our background. One of the biggest benefits of stretching is that it forces you to connect with your breath. In order for you to deepen into your stretch, you have to take a deep breath and exhale as you push a tiny bit deeper each time. Doing this actually gives you better control of stress levels and helps to correct bad habits when it comes to your posture.

Just improving your posture can have so many benefits like:

- Increased Confidence
- More Energy
- Higher Self-Esteem
- Better Mood
- Boosted Productivity
- Better digestion
- Less head, neck, and lower back pain - especially for those of us at a computer all day

Once it becomes a habit to control our breathing through discomfort, it can have a domino effect on our well-being and our overall health by lowering our anxiety and stress levels, leading to more energy, mental clarity, and focus.

Recently, I noticed that a new client of mine was having a hard time with mind-body connection and being present in the present. I had her meet me in the gym so I could assess her relationship with her body and figure out how to get her connected in a deeper way.

As we were warming up and cooling down, I noticed that she had a difficult time relaxing into a stretch and would tense up and shake, trying to force her body into submission.

I could see that her body was resisting and putting up a fight.

The minute I had her start to breathe into the stretch, instead of holding her breath, her body relaxed and stopped shaking. As she took a deep breath and filled her lungs, she lifted just enough out of the stretch to create space for her lungs to expand.

On the breath out, she would fall slightly deeper into the stretch, allowing her body to rise and fall with her breathing, instead of against it.

It was in this place she found peace. Even though she was twisted up like a pretzel, she was more relaxed than I had seen her in months because she was finally connecting with her breath and her body.

I have been told that yoga isn't as much about the movements as it is about occupying the attention of the mind and body so that our spirit can be present.

Sometimes it's not about the act itself, but the experience that it opens up for us.

Chapter Five

GROUNDING

It must have been over 100 degrees out, but that didn't matter. The cool water splashed off of my horse's back and my bare toes dug deeper into the mud as I rinsed off the sweat from the morning ride. I was only ten years old, but I'd been comfortable on a horse since before I could walk. My childhood was spent away from the rest of the world, horseback riding, digging in the dirt, climbing fences, and feeding the squirrels before my dogs would come and chase them away. I had a freedom then that was so innocent and safe. I wasn't scared of anyone or anything;

I think back to that now—so much joy, so much love. Connected to the earth and nature in a primal way that fed my soul and gave me life, without even realizing it.

I use that memory now to center and connect back to the feeling of being fully grounded when I cannot get outdoors for whatever reason.

I may not be going out to bathe a horse anytime soon, even though I would love to, but I can find something similar.

There are so many ways to connect and ground to the natural energy of the world around you.

Earlier today, like most mornings and most evenings, I went outside barefoot to water the one hundred and something tropical plants and succulents I have in the tiny side yard of my 1400-square-foot home. It's not a big space by any means, but I have filled every nook and cranny I can, creating my own tropical oasis to escape to in the suburbs of Riverside, California. Standing in my oasis this morning, the cool soil cradled my bare feet and nestled in between my toes, sending tingles up my body. I could feel the sensation from my feet all the way up to the hairs on my head.

In these moments, the rest of the world falls away and I am connected to the earth, allowing its energy to flow through me and align my mind, body, and spirit.

The simple act of feeling the dirt or grass under your bare feet and the morning sun on your face can transform your anxiety to peace in a matter of minutes.

There is something childlike and playful about getting your hands and feet dirty, and in those moments of play, we can find joy.

If you are sitting there thinking, *Oh I am not going outside barefoot,* maybe it's time to take a look at that resistance. What is stopping you? Are you afraid your feet will get dirty?

Here's a simple tip: Bring out a towel with you to wipe your feet afterwards. Problem solved.

When we connect to the simplest, most basic part of life, we can connect to who we truly are. We are of nature. The closer we can connect to that, the closer to ourselves we will be.

Proven benefits of grounding:[1]

- Reduce inflammation and inflammation-related disorders
- Reduce or eliminate chronic pain
- Improve sleep and promote a deeper sleep
- Increase energy and vitality

---

[1] https://www.ncbi.nlm.nih.gov/pmc/articles/PMC3265077/.

- Lower stress and promote calmness in the body by cooling down the nervous system and stress hormones
- Normalize the body's biological rhythms
- Thin the blood and improve blood pressure and flow
- Relieve muscle tension and headaches
- Lessen hormonal and menstrual symptoms
- Dramatically speed healing time and help prevent bedsores
- Reduce or eliminate jet lag
- Protect the body against potentially health disturbing environmental electromagnetic fields (EMFs)
- Accelerate recovery from intense athletic activity

Even if I experience just one of these benefits, the dirty feet are worth it.

Chapter Six

MEDITATION

Now, let's be real. I'm not going to ask you to take a trip to an ashram to meditate and pray for days on end.

You don't have to go out and get singing bowls or chimes or crystals (even if I do love them and use them myself at times).

I am simply suggesting that you take just a few minutes each day—whether it is first thing in the morning, mid-day, or before you go to bed—to be still.

To allow your mind and body to connect, balance, and align.

You can listen to an audio as you are guided through a mindful journey, you can play soft music and focus on your breath, or you can even sit in the quiet and listen for whatever comes up.

One of my favorite ways to meditate, besides guided meditations, is to think of a time when I was grounded to nature. When I was most connected to my true self. When I was experiencing something that brought me joy or peace.

I think of the smells, sounds, and colors of that memory and I immerse myself in it.

I will sometimes remember the deafening sound of the waterfall and the mist on my face during a hike while visiting family in Big Timber, Montana. I remember a day at the beach with the sun warm on my skin and my feet dug deep into the cool sand below the surface. I remember riding my horses with an old friend, laughing with the excitement of jumping streams on a trail ride in the hills behind my old house, and a scuba diving trip on the backside of Catalina, where I saw more color in one place then I knew could exist in nature. All memories I relive in as much detail as possible to connect me back to the exact feelings of those experiences. And I am transported.

Meditation doesn't have to be done any certain kind of way. It just needs to have the ability to bring you peace and connect your mind, body, and spirit.

When you're fully aligned, you are more capable of fully honoring your own wants, needs, and desires.

I was actually surprised to learn that prestigious medical groups like the Mayo Clinic believe that the emotional and physical benefits of meditation can help you to:

- Gain a new perspective on stressful situations
- Build skills to manage your stress
- Increase self-awareness
- Focus on the present
- Reduce negative emotions
- Increase imagination and creativity
- Increase patience and tolerance
- Lower your resting heart rate
- Lower resting blood pressure
- Improve sleep quality[2]

Even if meditation only helped you with a few of the things listed above, I think it would be worth it. Don't you?

---

[2] https://www.mayoclinic.org/tests-procedures/meditation/in-depth/meditation/art-20045858.

Chapter Seven

JOURNALING

Settle into a quiet space. Notice any tension that comes up in your body and breathe love and understanding into and through it.

Continue to keep your breath deep and strong and start to get curious.

Take a sheet of paper and draw a line down the center.

On one side, write "Going Well." On the other side, write "Not Going Well."

To begin, I want you to choose the first area in your life that you feel needs a little (or a lot of) attention.

For the sake of the example, I will choose "Health."

On the first side, write what is going well with your health. Get specific.

Then on the second side, write out what isn't going well. Again, be specific.

Depending on where you are in your journey, you can use this in multiple areas of your life. What is going well with your health? What's not? What about your finances? Your relationships? Your career? Or your home environment?

You can look at all of the different areas of your life with this same method. Get curious and get connected.

Once you have things listed out, go deeper.

Some ideas of what to write about would be to describe what you would like to be experiencing instead of what isn't going well. What would that be like? Why is it important to you? What are you willing to commit to in order to make it happen?

This journaling exercise has helped countless clients identify what wasn't working, so they could start figuring out what would.

Chapter Eight

TAPPING[3]

Okay, so out of everything I have suggested thus far, this one takes the prize for most awkward. Why? Because you are literally tapping your face and body to connect you to the present moment.

While I am all for fun and play, doing this in front of other people had me a little skeptical to say the least.

What I will say is that over time, I have come to realize that it is an incredible tool to take the power from old limiting beliefs that I have been identifying with for way too long.

I can hear the voices of adults from my past and peers from my present chiming away at what they believe I am and I am not capable of: "Jenn, you're too loud. You're too much. You are just a know-it-all. You talk too much. You're just a loser drop-out, who do you think you are to do this work? You don't know enough. No one will read your book."

Tap, tap, tap that shit away.

For me, tapping started out as a love-hate relationship. When I tell you I found it weird and uncomfortable, that is putting it lightly. It was one of the most ridiculous things anyone had asked me to do

---

3   https://www.healthline.com/health/eft-tapping#:~:text=Proponents%20say%20the%20tapping%20helps,balance%20to%20your%20disrupted%20energy.

up until this point in my lifestyle recovery. But I knew if I was going to become a different kind of strong, I had to get comfortable doing uncomfortable things. So, I followed along.

The Emotional Freedom Technique (EFT) practitioner I hired to work with me asked me what limiting beliefs I was coming to her to help clear. I had done enough work with a coach at that point to know that my biggest limiting belief was that I didn't have the coveted degree I thought I needed in order to be successful.

As we began tapping, she had me repeat over and over again, "Even though I don't have a degree, I have what I need to be as successful as I want to be already inside of me."

Now, I didn't believe this at first, of course, but by the end of the session, not only did I feel comfortable with tapping, I felt relieved of the expectations I had put on myself by the rest of the world.

I had escaped the walls of the box those adults and peers had crammed me into and whenever I started to try to climb back in, I would start tapping and re-align with what was true for *me* instead.

We all have limiting beliefs. Stories that we tell ourselves are true, based on someone else's narrative. We have to release these in order to experience the life that we were meant to.

Sign into the book portal and get weird with me and one of my book's expert contributors as she walks us through the Emotional Freedom Technique: Tapping.

Chapter Nine

EXERCISE/ PURPOSEFUL MOVEMENT

When I tell you that exercise saved my life, I'm not exaggerating. During my six-month stay in rehab, the mental health counselors and therapists were trying to use different types of cognitive and behavioral therapy to help us break through some of what was keeping us stuck.

They kept asking us to identify feelings that would come up, to describe them, and give them a name. But all I could feel was the pulse in my face as my psych meds kicked in, and I started to zone out.

Here I was, in the place that was supposed to teach me how to cope, how to heal, and how to deal with the feelings that came up as I navigate life, but there was nothing there. No feelings to be felt, no tears to shed, no joy, no anger, no excitement.

I was just existing.

I knew that if I wanted to get the most out of my time there, I needed to learn how to feel *without* medication. I needed to be in a safe place to test the waters and deal with whatever came up as years of numbing, running, and disconnecting were certain to come flooding to the surface as repressed emotions began to creep in.

I knew what I needed to do. I needed to get off the meds.

I wish I could say my doctor, therapist, and parole officer were all on the same page, but that would be total bullshit.

It was actually a stipulation of my parole that I be medicated, because according to my record, I was a risk to myself and others.

But I was relentless and fought the decision all the way. It was the first time I ever really remember fighting for something I knew I needed, even if everyone else told me I was wrong.

I may not have realized it at the time, but this is where I started to become a different kind of strong. This is how I began to create a life I love and that I look forward to waking up in—by standing up for what I needed *regardless* of what anyone else thought was right for me.

Over the next month, I almost gave up. It would have been so much easier to get back on my meds, numb everything, and make everything that was happening to me go away. It was connection that scared me.

I was coming out of my skin, detoxing off of several antidepressants, mood stabilizers, and benzodiazepines. I could barely function.

In the common room, after programming one day, I couldn't take it anymore.

I had to move my body somehow. I had to get all of this nervous energy out. I was technically still a ward of the state, so it wasn't like I could just go outside for a run.

I felt so trapped that I contemplated making a run for it.

Would they catch me?

Of course they would, but how long would it take?

I wonder who works tonight . . .

Then, out of the corner of my eye and for the first time in the month that I'd been there, I spotted an old treadmill in the back of the room. I stepped up onto the old, rickety machine and turned it on. As the belt began to turn, the smell of burnt rubber filled the room and the screeching of the belt began to pierce our ears. But I didn't care.

If you have never heard an old treadmill screech, let's just say I fought off death stares for the next thirty minutes as I walked off the years of pain, anger, fear, resentment, and guilt that poured out of me.

Much to my housemates' dismay, I got on that old, loud, rickety-ass treadmill every single day for the next five months until I was released.

Once I was home, I started jogging outside every day, then started running, and eventually found a local twenty-four-hour gym that I could afford and began lifting weights.

The strength I began to build in the gym spilled over into all the other areas of my life. I worked harder in my business, took better care of myself, went back to school to get certified as a personal trainer, started a bootcamp, and even in the beginning of my fitness journey, I knew this would become a permanent lifestyle for me.

Since then, I have trained hundreds of clients, competed in dozens of bodybuilding and fitness competitions and I know without a doubt, I wouldn't be who I am today if I hadn't created the relationship I did with purposeful movement from the very beginning.

Mind-body connection is everything.

Pause and Reflect

Stop for just a moment and try something with me.

As you sit there reading this, I want you to center yourself with some deep breathing.

As you begin to settle into your body, I want you to get curious.

Where do you feel strong in your body?

Where do you feel weak?

Where do you feel tight?

Where do you feel flexible?

Where do you need relief?

Now ask yourself what that part needs from you?

What does it need you to do?

Stretch? Go for a walk? Breath more throughout the day?

Eat less sugar and more veggies?

Drink more water?

What does your body need from you right this minute?

Listen for the answer because you instinctively know, even if you haven't been doing it . . .

Then do it.

You are worth the effort, my friend. I promise.

Chapter Ten

GARDENING[4]

During my stay at CIW (my second term in prison), our units were inspected every Friday.

This meant that the yard crew had to make sure every weed was pulled, every plant was trimmed, and all the leaves were raked up. It had to be picture-perfect along with the inside of our unit, because first place during inspection got to shop first that week. Things run out very quickly on limited supply, so it's a pretty big deal. If you wanted to get certain flavors of ramen soup, the newest shampoos or body washes, or limited supply type items, being first was absolutely vital.

I'm proud to say, our unit shopped first *every* week.

One day the yard crew was short and I was asked to help. Until then, I had never gardened or had anything to do with plants. I followed behind a coworker for the first few hours, asking questions, raking the dead leaves she had pruned off some plants. As I watched her work, I could see a sense of peace and contentment come over her that I didn't know was possible in a godforsaken place like prison.

---

[4] https://www.barefoothealing.com.au/v/what-is-earthing/22#:~:text=To%20put%20it%20briefly%2C%20when,and%20disease%20in%20the%20body.

But there she was, in her mid-fifties, twenty years into a life sentence without the possibility of parole, humming and smiling, getting her knees and hands dirty with seemingly no care in the world.

What was this sorcery? I needed to know what meds she was on 'cause she had to be high.

I asked her why she seemed so happy.

She didn't even look up at me, but without skipping a beat she replied, "I may be powerless over *where* I live, but I am not powerless over *how* I live. I can choose to get caught up in the drama in this prison, or I can choose to find the joy and beauty in things. Gardening, nurturing something throughout its life, pruning, watering, and watching it grow, gives me life and brings me joy. When I am with these plants, with my hands digging in the earth, I am not in prison. I am free."

From then on, my hands were in the dirt every single day. It was my new escape, but this was different. This time I wasn't so much escaping as I was connecting to the earth and releasing the fear and insecurities of the outside world that had plagued me for so long.

When I was gardening, I was at peace.

Little did I know, there is a shit-ton of science supporting the fact that gardening, touching the earth with our bare skin, actually shifts our DNA.

To put it briefly, when your bare feet or skin come in contact with the earth, free electrons are taken up into the body. These electrons are nature's strongest antioxidants and help neutralize the damaging free radicals that lead to inflammation and chronic disease in the body.

The earth's energy can actually shift our physiology, encouraging the body to heal and repair itself, promoting well-being, vitality, and better sleep. It also stabilizes the body's basic biological rhythms, knocks down chronic inflammation and its associated pain, making it the most natural and powerful anti-inflammatory and anti-aging remedy around! No matter what your age, gender, race, or health status, you will benefit from a daily dose of touching the earth.

An easy way to start is by growing your own herbs or even buying seed starter kits online.

It doesn't have to be difficult; it just needs to get your hands dirty.

Chapter Eleven

MIRROR WORK[5]

The most effective self-compassion exercise I have ever experienced was mirror work.

Mirror work is exactly what it sounds like. It involves gazing at yourself in the mirror while saying positive affirmations such as "I love myself," "I am strong," or "I am capable."

Let's try it now.

Get up from wherever you are and go find a mirror.

Stand directly in front of the mirror and look straight into your own eyes.

This may be super uncomfortable, so if you need to, stop here the first few times and just get used to actually looking into your *eyes* instead of at every other possible place to look. Keep repeating this every single day until you can take the next step.

Once you are able to look yourself straight in the eyes, allow whatever negativity that comes up to only linger for a moment, then out loud, tell yourself, "I love you and you are worth it."

Repeat this five times.

Do this practice daily, changing up the phrase if you'd like:

---

[5] https://www.mindbodygreen.com/articles/mirrorwork#:~:text=Mirror%20 work%20involves%20gazing%20at,if%20just%20for%20a%20moment.

"You are worthy of holding space."
"Your feelings are valid."
"You are capable of anything you put your mind to."

Confusing emotions can come up while doing this. Be kind and patient with yourself and remember to stay out of judgment.

The practice was created by self-love expert Louise Hay, who wrote *Heal Your Body*, as well as *Mirror Work: 21 Days to Heal Your Life*, in which she exclaimed that "doing mirror work is one of the most loving gifts you can give yourself."

There are so many benefits to incorporating mirror work into your personal growth journey.

Strengthening connection to yourself.

When you are standing there, staring in the mirror with no one else around, it's just you; all of you. No other opinions, no other input, just you—what you think and how you feel. You are able to begin to really see yourself through your own eyes.

Boosting your self-esteem.

Being in front of the mirror can be crazy uncomfortable, especially if you struggle with low self-esteem. But as the negative self-talk starts to creep in, you can state positive affirmations out loud and directly to the person in the mirror, and chances are you'll slowly but surely start to believe them. Maybe not at first, but with consistent effort, you may even learn to love the person you see.

Overcoming insecurities.

As you continue to do mirror work, the consistent affirmations to yourself, from yourself in front of the mirror can eventually help you break through the embedded negative self-talk.

Healing your inner child.

If you're curious about inner child work, or healing the old wounds from childhood, mirror work is a great practice to incorporate. By continuing to focus on overcoming insecurities and deepening your connection with yourself, the old stories from your past begin to shift. You begin to notice who those voices actually belong to and can determine if they are really true for you, or not.

Becoming self-assured.

Last but not least, mirror work can help you increase confidence and self-assuredness. Rather than looking outside yourself for emotional support, praise, love, and even compliments, you can fill your own cup and nurture yourself into the healthy, happy life you deserve. When you learn to trust yourself, it opens up an entire world of possibilities. You begin to imagine a life for yourself you never believed was possible before.

No matter how you connect to the present moment, do it with love, compassion, and curiosity.

Leave the judgment off the table.

If you start to notice yourself thinking mean or hateful things, I want you to ask yourself if you would say that to another person you loved.

If you wouldn't say it to them, why would you say that to yourself?

Love on yourself the same as you would love on them.

That's where the magic happens.

Chapter Twelve

GETTING CURIOUS

All right. I'll admit it. The hardest part of all of this really is the actual implementation.

Only 8 percent of people actually follow through with their New Year's resolutions.

Why is that?

Over the years, it has literally been my mission to figure out *why* we say we want something, then in the end, give up going after it when unforeseen circumstances arise or it gets a little complicated.

Of course it's going to get complicated.

Everything you have done up until this point, whether you recognize it or not, has been for a reason.

That extra weight? There's a reason.

That dead end job . . . a reason.

That relationship that makes you feel like shit about yourself? Yep, you've got it.

There's a reason you've kept these parts in your story for so long.

Now, of course I am not a therapist, and even if I was, I don't know your story.

But chances are, you have been convincing yourself that something is true that just isn't anymore, and we need to figure out why.

What I have learned is that we tell ourselves stories to keep ourselves safe.

But Jenn, I'm not scared of reaching my goals!

You may not realize it, but some part of you must be. Even if it's a small, unrecognizable part, it is causing you to sabotage yourself one way or another. Often this can come from repressed trauma or unresolved emotional abuse.

Maybe you want to start your own business, but you are struggling to believe you can be successful. The story you tell yourself is that it's too hard, takes too much time, and you can't fit it into your current life. So you start doing busy work to prove you don't have the time.

The truth is plenty of men and women have gone to school while working a full-time job and raising kids.

They figured it out and so can you.

You just haven't found the right strategy for you.

When we doubt ourselves, we don't move forward because of fear of what might happen if we actually went all in.

What if I put in 200 percent and I fail?

What if I invest all this money and don't follow through and it's just a huge waste?

What if no one else sees value in what I have to offer?

But what if they do?

It can be scary to believe in something when you have no evidence.

But what is faith?

It is trusting in something even when you can't see it. It's believing in your own truth instead of what others think is right for you. It's defying what the world has taught you to believe and choosing a path that may be different from what has been laid out for you.

Up until now, I believe you have tried to do "the right thing" for you and your family. I believe that you have been trying to figure out the answer to why you are stuck in a rut and can't seem to get your health, business, or relationship to the next level.

I believe that you have had nothing but positive intentions. But having a positive intention is completely different than having a good strategy.

Chapter Thirteen

INTENTIONS VS. STRATEGY

The very first time I was ever asked what *I* wanted, my perspective was so skewed by my past that I never could have imagined wanting the life I have today.

It didn't just come to me one night in a dream; it was years of trying and failing—or more appropriately trying, learning, and adapting.

When we supposedly "fail" at something, what do we make that mean about ourselves?

For me, I've learned that if I try my best and I still don't meet the goal I had set for myself, that means I get to adapt.

In science there is no such thing as failure. A science project never fails. There is always data and information acquired to carry to the next experiment—always.

So whether you call it an opportunity for adaptation or you call it data . . . there is no such thing as failure.

Looking back now, I can recognize that I had the best of intentions in the early years of my recovery.

But good intentions are different than having a good strategy.

My original intention has always been to help people find their own personal freedom, to be able to feel comfortable in their skin, to feel confident holding space for themselves, and using their voice. To have the courage to go after what they want, no matter what anyone else tells them they are capable of. To stand up for who they are and live authentically without guilt or shame. To build up the strength inside of themselves that they never knew existed.

My initial strategy was to do that by giving them the perfect meal plan and training routine. I thought that if they could feel strong and confident, then they would go after everything they wanted in life.

The intention was great. The strategy . . . not so much.

What I learned over time was that I didn't know what was best for my clients.

I could write them a meal plan all day, but would they actually follow it?

What was their relationship like with food?

With their body?

With the gym?

What I realized was that it wasn't my job to just *tell* them what to do. It was my job to *ask the right questions* and help my clients find their *own* right answers.

What *their* body is supposed to look like.

What foods *their* body likes to eat.

What brings *them* joy.

What success means to them.

What *their* love language is.

What *they* need in *their lives* to feel whole and complete, lacking nothing.

Instead of what everyone else has told them they should be, think, or feel their entire lives. Including me.

I had amazing intentions . . . but I knew I needed a better strategy.

Did I help women get stronger with the workouts I took them through? *Yes.*

Did I help women feel more confident? *Yes.*

Did some clients compete and win shows? *Yes.*

Did more than most fall back into old patterns the minute they stopped working with me?

Absolutely, without a doubt, yes.

Why?

Because you can't make a permanent shift in your habits if you don't identify and get to the origin of your old stories and beliefs. They are the main reason why you continue to default to your old lifestyle patterns.

If you want to build a healthy relationship with food and your body, you can't continue to live in the diet culture that created your food insecurities in the first place (recovering orthorexic[6]).

If you want to launch a business, you can't keep waiting for things to be perfect before you put your services out there (recovering perfectionist[7]).

If you ever want to live an authentically happy life of personal, emotional, and financial freedom, you can't say 'yes' to everyone before you say 'yes' to yourself (recovering codependent[8]).

You simply can't build a skyscraper on sand.

In the beginning of my coaching journey, I was mostly working with women who wanted to change their bodies. As a trainer, the only tools I had were food plans and workouts.

As I built my skills as a coach, I started to get curious about why my clients were so strong-willed in front of me, but would lose any sense of accountability once they walked out of those gym doors.

---

[6] Orthorexia is an unhealthy focus on eating in a healthy way- webmd.com.

[7] Perfectionist-a person who refuses to accept any standard short of perfection- Google dictionary.

[8] Codependency is a dysfunctional relationship dynamic where one person assumes the role of "the giver," sacrificing their own needs and well-being for the sake of the other, "the taker." https://www.psychologytoday.com/us/basics/codependency.

I started to realize my curiosity was coming from a much deeper place.

Let's say you have just signed up with a trainer to lose "*X*" number of pounds.

You invest the money, are given a nutrition plan to follow along with the workouts, and have every intention of following through this time.

Yet, before long, you catch yourself standing in front of and staring into an open cupboard or a fridge, searching, overlooking the food you have that is prepared and ready to be eaten, hoping something else that you actually want is going to magically appear.

But nothing does and you just get frustrated, slam the door, and grab a bag of whatever is in the snack basket on your way back to the other room.

Then, without fail, you are "mf'ing" yourself all over the place for failing again.

See, what was the point?

It wasn't going to work . . .

You were just going to fail anyway.

All the negative self-talk kicks in and before you know it, you go ahead and finish the bag of whatever you already mindlessly ate half of, that you swore you wouldn't eat in the first place.

This is where we get to stop and take a breath.

What if, instead of you being a judgmental asshole to yourself, you simply got curious.

What was the positive intention of ignoring the meal plan and going for comfort food?

What if you were hungry for something that you can't actually eat, like comfort, personal gratification, joy, or even a low-key need to be rebellious?

Your positive intention may have just been to find some peace or pleasure, which every single one of us needs and deserves to have in our lives.

When you constantly deny yourself your own time and attention, you are bound to sabotage and disconnect one way or another.

If instead, you shift your focus and get curious, you can check in and get clear about what you really want and adjust your strategy.

Maybe, if you are looking for comfort, you could turn off the ringer on your phone, curl up with some yummy tea, and a good book? Or call up a friend to meet for coffee? If you are seeking personal gratification, you could work on a favorite hobby or tend to your garden—which has the added bonus of connecting you to the earth. Joy could be found in taking a walk and breathing in the fresh air. As for the rebellion, how much more rebellious could you be than by going against your limiting beliefs and sticking to the plan for your dream life?

You intrinsically know what you want.

Sometimes we just need to sit in the discomfort of not knowing a little bit longer and ask ourselves what that really is.

What do we really want?

When you take a deep breath and connect to your current experience, you are allowing yourself the opportunity to pause and get curious around the actions you take that are either aligning you with or sabotaging your goals. Find the positive intentions and create a strategy to fulfill the intention that better aligns with where you want to go.

PART TWO

ALIGNMENT

Chapter Fourteen

FUTURE PULL

2017

Someone once asked me, "If I look at your schedule each day, would I know where you want to be in ten years? Would I be able to tell what your goals and aspirations are?"

Well, shit. Would they?

The more I thought about the question, the more uncertain I got.

Up until that point, I was taught that by just taking the next indicated step, I would automatically align with what I wanted—that things would just fall into place the way they are "supposed to."

But, as I sat back and really thought about it, I didn't know if that was 100 percent the case.

I had the best of intentions and I was taking a ton of action with training clients and helping people learn how to eat and train to lose fat and build muscle, but was my strategy in alignment with where I really wanted to go?

With what I really wanted for myself or my clients?

I had competed in over fifteen fitness competitions over the course of seven years. I had a full personal training clientele, prepped women for their own competitions, and was helping hundreds of women change the way they looked and felt about themselves.

But was I actually helping them become the *best* they could be?

I may have been helping them change their bodies, but how did they *really* feel about themselves?

Who were they being when they weren't with me in the gym—the other twenty-three hours of the day?

Who were they being when they looked in the mirror?

When they got cut off by another driver?

When their coworkers piled it on them because they'd do the work without a fight?

Who were they being in their day-to-day lives?

Shit, who was I being?

Was I actually making the kind of difference in their lives I thought I was?

Was I actually being an example of what it looked like to make my own health, happiness, and success a priority?

Did I really want these women to follow in *my* footsteps?

The truth was, I wasn't doing as well as everyone thought I was.

I was miserable and judgmental of myself and others. I was counting and measuring every bite of food I ate, in the gym working out two-three hours every day, never going out with friends or seeing my family, and my only social life was on social media.

I was always trying to prove myself worthy of success, but what was my idea of success?

Was it getting my professional title as a competitor?

Was it having the perfect body?

Was it helping other women to "get the perfect body"?

What did that even really mean?

Perfect according to *whom*? The judges who happened to be at the show that day? People on social media? The audience at the competitions?

Me?

I thought back to that moment on stage at my last competition. My coach at the time had seen what I couldn't.

While I was proud of myself for reaching my goal, I wasn't happy. I wasn't in alignment.

I wasn't on the path I needed to be on, in order to get where I wanted to go.

I'll never forget her telling me after practice one day, a few weeks before my last competition, "It doesn't matter what you think other people want from you. What matters is what you want from yourself. You must follow your heart."

Her words reverberated in my ears.

I met Oksana Grishina when I was working, doing live interviews at the 2016 Los Angeles Fitness Expo.

I felt an immediate connection to her and hired her to help me with my posing and creating a fitness routine for an NPC Fitness competition. We have been friends ever since. This woman is one of the greatest fitness athletes of all time, yet she is also the most kind and humblest woman I have ever met. Her beautiful, quiet strength makes you feel like you can be anything you want to be when she is behind you, cheering you on.

I wanted nothing more than to make her proud and I thought in order to do that, I needed to do well on stage. But, the truth was, whether I did well or not, she only wanted me to be happy. To fully pursue my dreams—whatever that looked like. She had become one of my biggest supporters and would back me no matter which direction I wanted to go.

But where did I want to go?

What did I want if it wasn't to compete?

Once again, I had disconnected and become something I thought everyone wanted me to be.

What I thought everyone needed me to be.

It was time for me to get crystal clear about what I wanted and where I was going . . . not just for myself, but for my clients.

It's like google maps. When we connect to our current experience, it's like plugging in our current location. Now I needed to plug in my desired location so I could figure out exact step-by-step directions to where I wanted to go.

I sat back in my chair, uncrossed my legs, and closed my eyes. I took some long, deep breaths to clear my mind and body and let my spirit be present.

I relaxed into my seat, flattened my feet on the floor, and wiggled a bit to shake off the nervous energy.

Then I began what's called a "future pull."

I imagined myself doing the same thing I was doing, a year in the future.

I imagined it as if I were there. Still in the gym, counting reps for clients, knowing damn well the minute they went off on their own, they'd dismiss their goals and fall back into old habits and patterns. I felt into the experience and noticed I was resentful and frustrated. It's hard to pour so much of yourself into something and know that it's going to waste.

I sat in the feelings for a bit to acknowledge them and give them some space.

I took some more long, deep breaths and shook off the impending doom of everything staying the way it was. I took a few more breaths and stepped into a *new* vision of myself a year from now.

This time, I was working with clients who wanted to make a shift in their lifestyles, not just their bodies. I was helping them to connect to what they really wanted in life and who they were being on a daily basis. I was teaching them to have compassion for themselves and how to hold space without tearing themselves down.

This.

This is what I wanted.

This is the work I wanted to be doing in this world.

I felt fulfilled. Purposeful. In complete alignment and excited about the impact I was making.

I didn't know how, but I knew that my journey was about to head in a completely different direction.

I was going to make sure of it.

If you are reading this right now and you are fifty thousand dollars in debt, in a dead-end job, or working yourself to death with no time for yourself or any possible light at the end of the tunnel, I've been there. It's going to be pretty difficult to envision yourself crazy successful, owning some incredible home in the place you've always wanted to live, in a relationship with the person of your dreams, and in a thriving career that feeds your soul, but believe me when I tell you, it's 100 percent possible.

You just have to be able to imagine it first.

Pause and Reflect

What is something you can only imagine having come true for you in your life?

Where would you live? What would your home be like? What would you do for a living? Would you retire early? How would your finances look? How many people would you help as a result of your wealth and abundance? What would your health be like? Where would you travel?

The trick to creating true alignment is to be honest about where you are right now in your life and to be *completely* honest about what you want life to look like for you in the future.

When I say completely honest, I mean 100 percent *your* vision. Not the vision your family, friends, professors, or colleagues see for you; what you see for *you* and *your* future self.

I want you to let go of all of the circumstances you think will hold you back—all of the reasons *why not*—and I want you to get super clear on *what if.*

What if your health was where you wanted it to be? *What if* you had more energy? *What if* you were debt free? *What if* you traveled once or twice a year?

Reflect back to the list we made in Part One: Connection, of things that are going well and things that aren't.

Before anything else, let's take a moment to be grateful for what is going well.

Even if it seems small, be proud of yourself for aligning these pieces of your life.

Remember, what we focus on, grows. Take just a moment, grab a sheet of paper and a pen, or just scribble in the white space on this page, and write down at least five things you are grateful for that are going well in your life.

If we want more of the good, we need to focus on the good. However, ignoring what isn't going well doesn't work either.

It is so important that who we are presently being and who we want to become are in alignment.

That means, the actions I am taking matter.

The thoughts I am thinking matter.

What I believe to be true matters.

The people I surround myself with matter.

That's why getting comfortable with connection *first* is so important. When we can get clear on who we are being in any given moment, we can decide if the actions we are taking are in alignment with who we want to be and where we want to go.

Now, let's take a look at what isn't going well.

If there are things on that list you don't want, then what *do* you want instead?

If you don't want to be in debt and you want to have savings instead, how much do you want in your bank account?

Now dig in and tell me, why? What will having that in the bank do for your future self? Why is it so important to eliminate your debt? Get specific.

If you don't want to hate your body, what do you want your relationship with your body to be like instead? Again, specifically, why? What will you be able to do when you feel comfortable in your body that you aren't doing now?

If you don't want to be burnt out, then what will you do when you have more energy? What will it look like in your daily life if you have the energy to do the things that bring you joy? What are those things?

Dig deep and really explore the reasons behind the things that you want for your life. The more clearly you can picture the destination, the more easily you can design the roadmap.

Pause and Reflect

See a pattern here?

What is coming up for you right now?

I invite you to take a moment and journal.
*Capture these thoughts in real time and connect
to them.*

When we get to the root of what we really want, we can connect to what it will feel like when we get there.

If I just tell myself I want something and don't really feel into the reason *why* I want it, it's just superficial, and there's a very small chance of it actually happening.

What actually can tend to happen, instead, is we revert back to our comfort zones and our old belief that it's too hard or takes too much time or that we can get to it after *X*, *Y*, or *Z*.

There is that part of us, trying to keep us safe. We think by playing small, we will be safe from outside judgment and criticism. Safe from failing or from looking like a fool.

The truth is, if I decided to play small, I definitely would have already given up.

If I was afraid of you judging me because I'm a felon or a drug addict, I never would have had the opportunity to impact countless lives.

If I was afraid of sounding dumb because I don't have a college degree, I never would have written this book.

I did all of it scared shitless.

I had to dig deep and ask myself *why* I *had* to do this, or I never would have kept going.

I may tell myself I want more clients, but if I don't take the time to connect to the reason why, I can easily tell myself that having more clients will be overwhelming and I won't be able to balance it.

I know that isn't true, but it is a limiting belief that could get in the way of me taking action. So, instead, I will connect to the fact that I want more clients because the more people I help, the more people they can help. I know that by serving more clients I will make an even bigger impact than I already have. I know if I make a bigger impact, more health and wellness professionals will learn how to set solid boundaries around their own personal health and mental wellness, so they can in turn, serve our communities better, for longer.

If I can embody the feelings I will have once I accomplish my goal, I can lean into that feeling and away from the old patterns keeping me stuck.

When I met my client, Katherine, she and I hit it off immediately. I was fresh out of rehab and she would call to check on me almost daily. To find someone who cared so much about someone they just met, to me was priceless.

However, I quickly realized that while she cared so much for everyone else, she cared very little for herself.

She spent all of her time making sure everyone else was okay, yet when it came to herself, she was always last on the list. Her mental, emotional, physical, and spiritual health were all suffering, and with twenty-two active years in a twelve-step program, she couldn't understand why.

She was completely disconnected and out of alignment. She had no balance or structure other than work and meetings, and it was making her miserable.

Eight years into our friendship, once I became certified as a health and life coach, she immediately started to work with me one-on-one.

Our main goal was to help her create time and space for herself in her life so she could do the things she loved like traveling and spending more time with family.

During a session one day, I suggested we do a future pull. She was hesitant at first, but she eventually agreed. To begin, we centered her breathing, and I asked her to imagine herself one year in the future as if she had already reached her goals and was experiencing the results of her efforts.

I asked her to describe what it was like now that she had more time and energy and was making her health and happiness a priority.

"Now that I have a healthy relationship with food and my body, I don't feel so stressed out all of the time. I have more energy and so I'm doing more things with my grandkids," she shared.

I gently nudged her to go deeper and asked her to imagine herself somewhere specific. "Where are you, specifically? What are you doing? Who are you with?"

"I'm spending the day making memories at Disneyland with my family. We are all laughing, taking silly photos wearing Mickey ears, tasting and smelling all of the yummy food all through the park, and probably getting sick on the teacup rides because of it. My grandkids will remember this forever, and honestly, so will I." She opened her eyes and looked right at me and exclaimed with more certainty than ever before, "Yes! That's what I want!"

In that moment, my client stepped right into that experience. She knew, simply by imagining, what it would feel like to spend a day laughing with her family. But notice, she didn't even have to do any of the work yet to have that feeling. All she really had to do was close her eyes to take herself there and put herself into the experience of having the results.

To make it happen, you have to *believe* it can happen.

In order to align with who you want to be, you have to be able to access that version of yourself—to check in with that part and decide if who you are *being* is going to help you get to who you want to *become*.

My client had never allowed herself to really imagine what it would be like to spend her time the way that she wanted, because it made her sad. Until we met, she didn't think it was possible to make that big of a change "at this age" and had given up any ideas of traveling and spending loads of time with her family.

Once she connected to that part of her that really wanted something, the parts of her that were scared didn't have as much power anymore.

She was able to step into *what if* and *what could be*.

Curiosity at its finest.

Chapter Fifteen

SETTING INTENTIONS

Another client, Kristy, signed up with me for personal training at the gym, long before I became a life coach.

When we first met, she was so caught up in "making it work" all of the time, that she couldn't see two feet in front of her.

She was constantly trying to manipulate situations so she could do the minimum and get the maximum return.

She had the best of intentions, but her strategy left something to be desired.

If you are good at math, you know that two minus four will never give you a positive result, yet day in and day out, she was taking two steps forward and four steps back, disappointed that she was falling further and further behind.

She would come to the gym, but not eat all day, so she wouldn't get any stronger. She wanted a healthy relationship with a man, but allowed her ex to live with her.

She wanted to build a business, but filled her spare time doing busy work that was not contributing to consistent business growth.

At the time, we both thought that if she could build her self-esteem, get stronger, and more confident, that it would get her on the path to success that she wanted to be on.

While it did help and she even went as far as competing in a bikini competition, it was still all superficial. Surface work.

I'll never forget her coming up to me after the competition and saying, "Well, that was fun. Imagine if I had actually done everything you said to do!"

I chuckled, not in amusement, but disbelief. I was actually beside myself.

Where was the integrity?

Didn't she know how much of myself I had poured into her?

Didn't she know I was basing my success off of hers?

Wait.

What?

Talk about a moment of clarity.

Her intention was to do something she'd never done. To challenge herself and to see what she was capable of.

She did that and she was proud.

But outside of that?

Of course I'd had the best of intentions. I wanted to help her feel confident, capable, and strong, which she did until after the show ended.

Ultimately, all competing in the show did was make her even more judgmental of her body, supported a weird relationship with food, made her obsessed with pinching her skin to see if her body fat had gone up or down, and was only focusing on the physical results.

She began scrolling social media and comparing her body to women who were twenty years younger, on performance enhancers, and had more work done to themselves than Mt. Rushmore.

I had turned her into me.

This was not what I wanted.

Over the next year, I slowly backed away from the gym as I began to resent counting out reps for my clients, when I knew I wanted to work with them on a deeper level. I knew I wasn't making the kind of impact I had been called to make, and I felt deflated.

In time, I eventually stopped training clients and even stopped training myself all together.

My food went from clean and organic to fast and processed.

My manic depression kicked into high gear and cemented me to the couch, disconnecting me from everyone and everything—including myself.

I was sick with the flu three times in six months, and prior to that I hadn't had the flu for as long as I could remember.

I was rotting from the inside out.

On the couch, scrolling mindlessly through Facebook one day, I saw an ad to become a certified health and life coach through the Health Coach Institute (HCI).

A health coach?

What, like some MLM supplement pusher who all of a sudden was a guru because they followed some processed food protocol or some fad diet plan?

Yeah, no thanks.

But those damn Google ads sure know when something catches your eye, don't they?

All of a sudden, the HCI ads popped up every time I opened social media. So, of course, curiosity got the best of me.

The truth was, the more I read, the more I realized it was exactly what I had been looking for.

Who knew health and life coaching was a real thing?

I couldn't help but identify with their target audience.

I was a wellness professional who wanted to know how to go deeper with my clients. I wanted to learn how to teach them how to shift what they believed to be true about the world and how they identified in it.

Actually, it was exactly what I needed too.

Deep in my gut, I knew this had been what was missing.

I wanted to be a coach. It was pulling at me more than anything had in as long as I could remember, but it was a $6000 investment and way more than I thought I could afford.

Until then, my relationship with money hadn't been all that great. I didn't care about making a lot of money or having high-end brands or a fancy car.

I cared about being of service. I cared about helping people transform their lives.

I hadn't been worried about making more than I needed to pay my bills and survive. My bank account didn't have much more than a few hundred in it at any given time since I'd been out of prison.

This was one of the first experiences where I realized, even if briefly, that if I made more money, I could help more people.

But it was a passing thought and it didn't matter at that moment. What mattered was that I had to figure out how to make it happen.

I may not have had enough money in the bank, but I didn't care.

I knew this was the exact shift that my clients needed from me, so I could help them reach that next level in their lives.

I was scared to make such a big investment in something so uncertain, but I did it anyway.

I knew something had to change.

Thank God for credit cards.

2018

I spent the next six months perfecting my craft. The moment we were cleared to work with clients, Kristy was my first call.

She was immediately on board and we began our coaching journey together, which actually ended up lasting for years.

Kristy went from scraping by day-to-day, doing the bare minimum, borrowing from everyone, even her ex (in her own words, "mooching" from everyone), to selling multi-million dollar homes in Marin, California; traveling the world; making her health and happiness a priority; going to the gym and for walks around her beautiful neighborhood; preparing and enjoying whole, clean foods; making real, deep connections; building friendships; dating men worthy of her time; and making the memories with her kids that she always dreamed of.

It didn't happen overnight, but she created this vision with me during our very first session in 2018, and here we are in 2022, and she is literally living as her future self.

Did either of us know it was going to happen?

Heck no.

She definitely had her doubts at times, wanting to give up and go back to what was familiar, but as her coach I continued to check in on her intentions and help her build a strategy that would work.

I continued to ask her if who she was being was who her future self needed her to be.

I continued to hold her accountable and hold space for who she was capable of being and I'll be damned . . . she did it.

Not only did she do it, but with continued support, she has continued to thrive in her life to this day—connecting and realigning, allowing her vision to shift and grow right alongside her.

We have to have a clear vision of where we are going, what we want, and who we want to be in order to stay in alignment and headed in the right direction.

Remember, I didn't start out on my fitness journey to look any kind of way.

It was for my sanity, for healing—to feel better in my own skin.

It was to be able to stay connected and grounded to my current experience without needing to disconnect and go numb.

It was how I learned to keep going, even when it hurt.

I had to reconnect, get crystal clear about my vision, and get back in alignment. Now I love my career and continue to grow and evolve with it every single day. I know, without a doubt, I am doing the work I was put on this earth to do.

That, for me, is true alignment.

Pause and Reflect

Are you in alignment with your goals?

Would your calendar show me where you want to be this time next year?

Grab the fillable daily planner over in the book portal to help you organize your schedule in a simple way.

PART THREE

BALANCE

Chapter Sixteen

CREATING SPACE

My alarm went off at 4:00 a.m., giving me just enough time to eat a meal, get dressed, take my supplements, and get to the gym for spin class at 5:00 a.m.

After spin, at 6:00 a.m., I raced home to work on marketing for my coaching practice before heading to the salon for a ten-hour day. I'd arrive home, grab whatever was easy and accessible in the fridge or cupboard, plant myself in front of the computer, and catch up on what I needed to with coaching.

When I couldn't see straight anymore, I'd roll into bed, pass out, wake up, and do it all over again.

I had no social life except for who I saw at the gym and I didn't really do much other than work, eat, and sleep.

That was fine for a while. In fact, I loved it. I felt busy and productive and successful.

Until I didn't.

Before long, I grew resentful. I wanted my freedom back. I wanted to experience life. I wanted to take a few days off and go somewhere.

I wanted to go out with my friends and have fun.

I wanted to quit living in this fear that if I stopped being so busy all the time, that it would all fall apart.

That I would fall apart—I honestly believed I would.

As someone who had already lost herself completely one too many times, the fear of going backwards loomed over me every single day.

I realized that living in fear of failure was a recipe for disaster.

This couldn't be what success felt like.

How could I feel free if I was constantly trying to prove my worth? If I was constantly trying to live up to some ridiculous standard I thought I had to live up to in order to be considered successful?

I had to decide for myself what success actually meant to *me*.

Was it having no time for friends? Or was it getting to spend plenty of time with friends and family?

Was it working sixty-hour weeks, or was it being able to schedule in ample amounts of downtime?

Was it finding a dead-end job for the guaranteed paycheck? Or was it running my own business and charging my worth?

I went back to the drawing board and took a look at my schedule. It was a mess. Back-to-back clients—not even a meal break. I was self-employed as a hair stylist and coach, so it was easy for the people-pleasing version of myself to overbook my time to fit others in and make them happy.

Was this really sustainable? Others did it.

In fact, it was kind of the norm. I mean, were you even successful if you could still stand at the end of the day?

I realized I had fallen into this pattern because it was what was accepted.

I didn't need to be accepted anymore; I needed to be able to breathe. I needed to be able to find a balance in my schedule that kept me in alignment with my goals, sustainably.

I pulled out my weekly planner and adjusted my booking schedule to add in some whitespace where I could, and from then on, meals, movement, and whitespace got scheduled *before* work and clients.

Whitespace in my calendar means that I have purposely scheduled out time to rest and recharge.

No calls, no emails, no writing, no work, not even working out or prepping food.

Whitespace means rest.

I purposely scheduled in time with friends and followed through.

I gave myself grace when I was too burned out from a ten-hour workday to go to the gym.

I allowed myself to have a cookie if I wanted a damn cookie. I scheduled out a week of vacation a few times a year, even if I didn't have anywhere to go. And slowly but surely, I began to figure out that it doesn't have to be all or nothing. That we are allowed to find a balance that works for *us* even if it doesn't fit into someone else's box.

The first ten years of my journey post-prison were a whirlwind.

I had so much on my plate.

Between continuing my education, still working in the salon, and starting up my coaching business, I was easily pushing a sixty-hour work week, going to the gym every day, finding time to take care of the house, and all of the adult responsibilities that went along with that. I was doing all the things that were supposed to make me a strong, responsible, productive member of society.

What didn't kill me was supposed to make me stronger, right? But I didn't feel stronger.

In fact, I felt like I was drowning.

I wanted to prove to myself and to the rest of the world that I could do this.

That I could take life head-on and win.

But I felt like I was failing miserably to keep it all together. Where was the fun? The joy? The play? It didn't exist.

I knew that I had been burning both ends of the candle, and if I kept on the way that I was, I was bound to burn out sooner than later.

If I didn't figure something out, there was no way I was going to be able to sustain this. So, I started googling:

"What do I do when I feel like I can't do it all?"

"Why can't I get through a whole day without crashing?"

"Why am I so tired all the time?"

What I found astonished me.

Did you know that 56 percent of healthcare workers quit within their first two years?

Fifty percent don't make it past five years.

This issue has also been exacerbated by the COVID-19 pandemic, as 95 percent of nurses have reported feeling burnt out within the past three years.

I realized right then and there, I had to make yet another shift. I needed to find a healthy balance between the life I had and the life I wanted.

I had to figure out what I needed to put in place so that no matter what was happening in the world around me, these things would keep me balanced, connected, and in alignment.

I refer to these habits now as my "non-negotiables."

Non-negotiables are actions or values that I have set in place in my life and my schedule that I do *no matter what*. No matter how inconvenient it is, or whether or not it upsets anyone else, these are the things I need to do so that I can have the life I want.

A few of my non-negotiables:

Clean, whole food 80 percent of the time

Daily purposeful movement—even when I'm tired and don't feel like it

Breaks in my day—even when I'm busy (*especially when I'm busy*)

Solid boundaries with others (*yes, even family*)

Being honest—even if I don't think you'll like the answer

I know for a fact that when I either don't eat, or I eat foods that inflame my gut, I am not going to be a pleasure to be around (and that's putting it lightly).

My mood becomes short and irritable, I have absolutely no patience with myself or others, I am quick to snap, and undoubtedly will develop a headache and stiffness somewhere in my body. I disconnect and my decision-making skills go out the window.

How do I know that?

I noticed (by checking in with myself all the freaking time) that when I am hungry, I have a difficult time being present. For me, that is unsafe.

I had to be able to connect and decide if *who I am being* and *what I am doing* are in alignment with who I want to be and where I want to go, so that I can make adjustments where I need to.

This gives me a chance to notice what is out of balance in my life and where I can shift my energy to refuel.

Where am I directing most of my time and attention?

There is only so much energy. It cannot be created or destroyed, just transferred or displaced, so if you spend all of your energy and focus on only a few areas of your life, inevitably, the others suffer.

Have you ever taken on extra work at the office and noticed that you and your spouse start arguing more and feeling distant?

Or set a fitness goal and then notice that you're irritable all the time and don't have fun anymore?

Maybe you begin to focus so much on your new relationship and making sure they are happy, that you put back on that ten pounds you lost and don't know how it happened.

What the heck is that?

That is what happens when we focus too much in one area of our life and don't balance our time and energy appropriately.

Pause and Reflect

What areas of your life are getting the most energy and what are getting the least?

Are you balancing your schedule to give you enough downtime? Are you scheduling things that bring you joy?

Or are you running yourself ragged, making sure you have time for everyone except yourself?

What would it look like if you gave a little more time and energy to the areas that aren't getting enough attention?

Ask yourself these questions:

How much energy am I devoting to my health?

Is it enough to reach my goals?

How are the other areas of my life supporting that goal?

Am I still spending quality time with my family?

Am I still performing my best at work?

Am I still finding time to rest and recharge?

In the book portal, I've included a worksheet to help you discover your own non-negotiables and a bonus daily planner for you to use as a guide to create a balanced schedule you love.

Chapter Seventeen

BALANCING THE GUT
TO BALANCE THE MIND

I wasn't sure if I was going to dive into this in this book, but the more I thought about it, the more I knew I couldn't leave it out: mental health.

It is the basis of our life experience, isn't it? Right alongside physical, emotional, and spiritual health.

But even if we are in peak physical health according to our sad excuse for "medical standards," we can still suffer from mental health issues.

As of today, the United States lacks any real preventative healthcare standard. Instead, we rely on what is known as a "Medical Management System."

What that means is, instead of teaching us how to prevent these chronic diseases, they won't help us until we already have issues that need to be *managed*.

With the amount of science that has been coming to the forefront about the direct correlation between gut health and mental health and how our lifestyle 100 percent affects our health, it is sadly all too clear that these "medical standards" are not in alignment with today's science and need some hardcore amendments.

Dr. Daniel Amen, author of *The End of Mental Illness* writes, "While medication is sometimes warranted, it should not be the first line of defense against mental illness."

For decades Dr. Amen and dozens of other doctors have written books, designed courses, and even created YouTube channels to share all of the science around healing your gut to heal your mind. Internal medicine specialist Dr. Mark Hyman has spent the last thirty-eight years working with and studying the effects of food on the gut-brain barrier. Functional medicine specialist Dr. Will Cole shares on his podcast all about the links between gut health and mental health. Dr. Steven Gundry, author of *Dr. Gundry's Diet Revolution*, created an entire protocol around what foods cause and reduce inflammation. I linked his specialized diet over in the book portal for you to use as a reference.

These are just a few of the revolutionary doctors who are transforming the medical industry and the way we associate gut health with mental health and neurogenesis.

Why hasn't everyone heard of them by now?

Here's the basics. Your gut has millions of neurotransmitters that send direct signals to the brain via the vagus nerve, which runs the length of our spine and connects to every single system in our body. This communication relies heavily on clear signals. When the gut is compromised from processed foods, sugar, artificial sweeteners, American gluten (yes, it's different here as our American food industry standards are sub-par to that of European countries) and other gut disruptors, it can allow pathogens and free radicals to break through the blood-brain barrier, enter the bloodstream, and wreak havoc on our brain and body systems.

Think of it like this: Your gut has a lining like a shag carpet. The purpose of the shag is to keep the large pieces of dirt and debris from getting through the netting underneath it.

When we eat an abundance of inflammatory, sugary, processed foods, it's like walking on the shag carpet with gum and mud all over our shoes. It messes up the shag and leaves large, unprotected areas of netting where large pieces of dirt and debris can get through. All that dirt and debris are just like those pathogens and free radicals getting through the lining of your gut into your bloodstream.

When that happens, your autoimmune response goes to war with the invaders and leads to most of the chronic diseases we know today.

It is actually the number one cause of chronic disease in our country.

According to the CDC, 51.8 percent of people in the United states suffer from at least one chronic disease[9] and 50 percent of people suffer from mental health issues.[10]

Think that's a coincidence?

Balancing the gut helps to balance the brain and reduce inflammation throughout the body, *including* the brain.

Some easy shifts you can make to help fortify your gut are:

Add in some fermented foods like miso, kimchi, kombucha, or yogurt

Prebiotic foods like garlic, onion, leeks, or asparagus

Adding probiotics into your supplement protocol

Cutting inflammatory foods like excess sugars, gluten, and dairy

Deep breathing before, during, and after your meal, as oxygen helps fuel digestion

---

[9] https://www.cdc.gov/pcd/issues/2020/20_0130.htm#:~:text=What%20is%20added%20by%20this,those%20living%20in%20rural%20areas.

[10] .https://www.google.com/search?q=what+percentage+of+the+us+population+suffers+from+mental+illness&rlz=1C1CHZN_enUS961US961&oq=what+percent+of+the+us+suffers&aqs=chrome.4.69i59j69i57j0i22i30l6.7503j1j7&sourceid=chrome&ie=UTF-8

Head over to the book portal for more gut health tips, including a curated list of proteins, fats, carbs, and supplements to help balance your gut and reduce inflammation so you can feel better and have more energy to focus on creating a life you love.

PART FOUR

BOUNDARIES

Chapter Eighteen

CHOOSING YOUR EXPERIENCE

Being an only child sucked. There's just no way around it.

I used to look around at my friends and their siblings, and no, of course they didn't always get along, but they were there. Always. A constant, built-in best friend. A confidant. A partner in crime. Someone to have your back or to argue with or to play or compete with.

But it was just me.

I sought validation from other kids my entire life, just wanting to fit in . . . to be liked and accepted.

So, I became who everyone else wanted me to be.

My parents loved me. That goes without question. I may not have understood it at the time, but I know they did.

They just showed it a little differently than other parents. Other parents said 'no' to their kids. Mine didn't. Mine loved me by always saying 'yes.'

I never knew what it was to want, let alone need. We went school shopping a couple times a year, had horses, cars, property, and anything I asked for . . . but none of it really meant anything to me.

I had come to just expect it. I had learned that if you loved someone, you gave them things.

You did things for them.

You didn't tell them 'no.'

My parents always said 'yes' and that meant they loved me, right?

My dad didn't have much growing up and so he wanted me to have more. He didn't want me to go without, so he gave as a way of providing. Providing for his family was everything to him.

The problem was I didn't appreciate any of it. I didn't know what it meant to go without, so I just expected that when I wanted something, I should have it.

The friendships I built over the years were so precious to me. If my friends ever needed me, I was there. Didn't matter what I had going on, I was there.

Drunk at a party? I'll drive. Failing a class? I'll do your work. Want to go to the movies, but don't have any money? Oh, I'll pay.

In fact, there wasn't anything I wouldn't do for my friends. Including serving time on charges that weren't mine, stealing for drugs, holding someone hostage, robbing a café. . . . There was literally nothing I wouldn't do, just to be liked or accepted by the people I was surrounding myself with.

It took losing everything, including myself, to realize that when you have nothing left to give, most friends disappear. It's the ones who truly matter who will still be there.

Not the ones who come running when they need you. But the ones who come running when they see you in need. The ones who know who you are and don't judge you. The ones who love you and put up with your crazy and who hold space for you to decide what is right for you in *your* life.

Luckily, after making some much-needed amends, I still had a few of those left. However, during my years of competing and fitness modeling, some of their lifestyles just didn't align with mine anymore. I felt like I was trying to force myself to fit in that old box again—like a plant that was rootbound and needed to be repotted so it had more room to grow.

Every weekend, a group of childhood friends would get together for a barbeque and any excuse to drink and celebrate. They'd start around noon and insist I come by after work. The problem was that by the time I'd get there, everyone would already be drunk, someone would be fighting, some would be overly emotional, and some would be trying to hang on to consciousness by the skin of their teeth, thinking they were just fine.

They were not fine and this was no fun for me.

I slowly stopped coming by, claiming that I had to work late or that I had other plans.

It worked for a while, but then they started to notice my absence. I started to be accused of being too good for them. Of thinking I'm better than them, simply because I didn't want to watch them get plastered every weekend.

The truth was it just wasn't fun for me. I didn't enjoy watching people get drunk and fight or cry all night.

So I did what I knew I needed to do and made it clear that I wouldn't be coming to any parties if I couldn't come at the beginning and enjoy everyone before it got crazy.

My true friends understood immediately. The ones who truly loved me and cared about me knew that their behavior wasn't healthy for me to be around. They supported me in my decision, and we decided on a few other ways to spend time.

But of course, there were those who took it as a personal affront when I stopped coming around. How dare I? Did I think I was better than them?

The truth was, not too long ago, I was in *prison*.

I had been an IV meth user, who was homeless on the streets. I had been less than nothing, yet here I was, putting boundaries on our friendships.

Who was I to judge them?

For a split second, hearing what their reactions had been to the news, I recoiled, believing they were right.

Who am I to judge?

But then, that part of myself that I had been nurturing, that best version of me found her voice:

"I am Jennifer Henry, damn it. I am the judge and jury of my own life. I am the only one who is responsible for deciding if something or someone is good for me in my life or not. If I don't judge whether or not someone is in alignment with where I want to go in life, how will I ever get there?

How do I honor what I need for myself? *My* health, *my* happiness, *my* well-being?"

And she was right.

I don't need to force my lifestyle on anyone and that's definitely not what I was doing, but by standing up for what was right for me, I challenged them and what they considered to be a successful life.

That was the problem.

They thought they had it all together and were living their best life.

That's fine and they may very well have been!

But that was not *my* best life. That was not how I wanted to spend my free time—disconnected, belligerent, and constantly seeking an escape from this reality.

I wanted to create a reality I *loved*. A reality I looked forward to experiencing and being present in.

Not one I was trying to escape.

Want to know the easiest way to lose any sense of self?

Say 'yes' to everyone.

People-please and burn yourself out doing all the things for everyone else.

Need to be needed, in order to be okay.

Find your worth in other people's opinions of you.

Rely completely on likes and follows on social media to validate your existence.

Never have an opinion.

Never hold space for yourself.

Never ask yourself how you really feel about something, and if you do, don't you dare voice it.

Don't listen to your body when it's telling you it doesn't like something.

Compare yourself to others and judge yourself for being different.

Copy every trend you see out there.

Mold your life according to what others view as success.

Want to live a joyful, authentic life of personal freedom?

Stop doing all of that shit.

Connect.

Get curious.

Be honest with yourself.

Hold space for every part of you.

Give every part a voice.

Let go of judgment and comparison.

Start allowing imperfection.

Stop being afraid of failure.

Trust that the highest version of you knows what he/she/it wants—and follow that intuition, even if it means upsetting others.

You are the only one who gets to decide what you want to experience in this life.

Chapter Nineteen

HONORING YOUR YESES AND NOS

December 2021

As I sat eating Christmas breakfast at the sparsely decorated dining room table with my fiancé, Michael, I looked across at the seats where my mom and dad had sat every Christmas morning since Mike and I had bought our first home four years prior.

They were empty.

The previous year had been during lockdown from the COVID-19 pandemic, and even then, we made sure to find a way to have Christmas breakfast together. But not this year.

Before I go any further, I want to say thank you, Mom.

Thank you for being so courageous in allowing me to share our story with the world, so that others may find the freedom and the healing they have been searching for, like we were for so many years. The generational curse is broken and I am so grateful for the relationship we've created. You are one of my best friends and you inspire me every single day.

I love you and I am so, so proud of you.

My mom was one of five daughters born to the clerk of a small town in Connecticut. Everyone in town knew my grandmother, Marge, so the sisters always needed to be on their best behavior. They knew the way they acted was an immediate reflection on their mother, and if she found out, especially if she had been drinking (which was the case more often than not), it could get ugly.

Mom was taught to be seen and not heard (and not seen if at all possible), speak only when spoken to, not to take up space, and not to have an opinion.

She quickly learned that if she played small, she was safe.

She grew up staying under the radar, and as she grew into an adult, she kept her head down and did what was asked of her without much argument or drawing any unnecessary attention.

When she moved all the way across the country to California in her late twenties and met my dad, I'm sure she thought it would be different. That she would become this free, outgoing woman who could take on the world and be her own person.

Why else would you move three thousand miles away to the other side of the continent?

It may have seemed like it was a huge change in the beginning, but as time went on, history began to repeat itself.

My dad, who is one of the best men I've ever known, is strong and loud and very opinionated. He carries himself as someone who knows more than most and can do anything he puts his mind to.

His confidence draws you in and makes you want to be around him. They fell in love and started a life together and in a couple years, they had me.

I was just as loud and opinionated as my dad (and as my grandma), so growing up, I always had a feeling that my mom was intimidated by me. Like I was too much for her to handle.

'Cause in many ways, I was.

My mom once said to me, "You know, we used to get along so well."

I asked her what happened and she replied, "You learned how to talk."

The answer hit me like a ton of bricks. No wonder we clashed.

I knew how to use my voice and that scared the shit out of her.

At this point I was eight or nine years into my healing journey and had done a shit ton of work around my relationship with my mom, but she hadn't seen a need to make any effort when it came to how she dealt with things.

In fact, she had become a pro at disconnecting from her emotions and her current reality, and her favorite tool to escape with was alcohol—a generational curse passed on by my grandmother.

As I grew and flourished in my lifestyle recovery, I watched my mom fade year after year. When COVID-19 hit, she was already hanging on by a thread.

My entire life, she had been John's wife and Jenn's mom.

She had no real identity, no friends, no hobbies, barely took care of herself, and when we went into lockdown, she would lie in bed and watch TV all day, miserable, lonely, and drinking herself to death. I cannot describe the feeling of watching someone slowly kill themselves right in front of you and there is nothing you can do about it.

My dad, always having been self-motivated and driven, didn't know what to do. He believed that she was a grown woman and could make decisions for herself. If this is what she wanted to do with her life, who was he to tell her she couldn't?

He knew from having gone through it with me ten years prior, that he couldn't help someone who wouldn't help themselves.

He was right.

But there *was* something he could do.

It was the same thing I had to do.

I had to set some *boundaries*.

I walked into my mom's bedroom a few days before Christmas.

It was one in the afternoon and she was still in bed. I could smell the alcohol coming out of her pores as she laid there, trying to figure out who I was and what I was doing in her room.

She began to mumble unintelligibly, saying something about how she was just about to get in the shower and that she was getting ready for her clients.

My mom had let her tax license lapse as a result of her drinking and no longer had any clients to speak of.

She was losing her mind right in front of me, a shell of her former, already meek self and there was nothing I could do or say to save her.

I realized right then exactly what I needed to do.

I couldn't stand by and watch my mom kill herself.

So I didn't. I told her I loved her and that she was a grown woman. If she wanted to continue to live this way, that was her choice. I had already done all I could by helping her find a sponsor and meetings to attend, calling and having a detox bed ready and waiting for her for weeks at a time, lining up rehabs, calling the rest of our family and getting their support.

None of it meant anything if she couldn't find a will to live. She was the only one who could decide if she wanted to live or die. She was the only one who could do the work.

I also knew that if she never had to suffer any consequences from her own actions, she would never need to change. Everyone would always be there to cosign her bullshit.

I couldn't do that anymore. I was drawing a line. Not just for her, but for myself.

I couldn't continue to be sick with worry every day. I couldn't keep feeling the need to disconnect from this pain. It was going to kill me right along with her.

As I left, I called my dad and I let him know that she wasn't welcome in my home this year for Christmas.

As much as I wanted them both to be there celebrating with me, I knew that if she came to my home the way she had been for the last year—slurring her words, falling all over herself, not making any sense, and not being able to look me straight in the face without going cross-eyed—I'd lose it.

I didn't have it in me. I needed to be completely honest with myself about that.

It was me or her, and after fighting for my life as hard as I had, I knew the choice I had to make.

I had to save my own life.

My dad struggled to understand how I could make such a decision, but I had to stand my ground.

It was by far one of the hardest things I have ever done, but I can do hard things.

2022

In February of the new year, I got a call that my mom had woken up in the morning with two broken teeth and a broken ankle and had no clue how any of it had happened.

I truly believed it was the wakeup call she needed to realize she was going to kill herself if she didn't make a change.

She signed herself into detox and stayed a week at Loma Linda Behavioral Health Center so they could get her vitals stable and a few days of real sobriety under her belt.

She said she was committed to continuing her journey in recovery and signed up for their intensive outpatient program.

Since she had a broken ankle, she couldn't drive herself, so my dad and I spent the next six weeks driving her back and forth, ninety minutes round trip in the morning and ninety minutes round trip at night, so she could get the help she *said* she so desperately wanted two cities away.

It was a Monday afternoon and I had a full day of clients when I got the call.

My mom had been admitted to the ICU, was intubated, sedated, and strapped down to a bed at Loma Linda University Hospital.

She had gone to the emergency room thinking she was having a panic attack, but it turned out she had been secretly drinking the entire time we were breaking our necks to drive her back and forth to treatment in Loma Linda.

Apparently, she had aspirated during a seizure that came on while she had been sitting in the waiting room, all because she was detoxing from alcohol that we didn't even know she'd been drinking.

I didn't know what to expect when I got there, but I could tell by my dad's voice on the other end of the phone call that it wasn't looking good.

I canceled the rest of my clients that day, jumped in my car, and broke every driving law in California to get there as fast as I possibly could. I burst through the double doors of the hospital, ignoring the calls from the nursing staff that I needed to sign in—and whatever else they were yelling at me that I couldn't care less about—and made my way directly to the ICU.

There she was, hooked up to more tubes than I could count, strapped down to her hospital bed because of unconsciously pulling at the tube that was down her throat breathing for her.

I watched as my mom lay there, thrashing in pain and wanting to come out from under whatever fog she was under, but unable to.

I watched my mom fight for her life every single day, thirteen hours a day, not knowing from one day to the next if she would ever wake up, ever remember who I was if she did. What if . . . what if she didn't want to come back?

What if this is what she had wanted all along? To be done with life? To not have to feel anything anymore? To permanently disconnect?

I knew the feeling all too well.

I couldn't think about that. All I could do was be there if and when she woke up, so I could find out.

Regardless of our past, regardless of our relationship up until that point, I loved my mom.

I knew enough about my own healing journey to know that whatever she decided was her choice.

Who was I to decide what she was meant to learn from her experiences in this life?

Who was I to decide that she had to fight?

This was her life and I continued to remind myself that all I could do was be an example of what it looked like to choose to live it.

All I could do was be the daughter to her that she didn't know she needed.

Four weeks passed as my mom lay there fighting for her life. She had been having seizures while under sedation, so even if she did wake up, there was no guarantee she'd fully come back.

What if this was it? What if I had cut my mom off and the last thing I remember was having to tell her she couldn't come to Christmas? Or that I couldn't be in her life?

What if this was my doing? What if this was all my fault? What if I had handled the situation differently? If I had just let her be belligerent and been okay with it, would it have turned out differently?

As painful as it was to admit to myself, I realized I would do it all over exactly the same way. My mom made her own choices. She made her own decisions. She is a grown woman and I didn't need to feel guilty for letting her suffer her own consequences.

I knew it wasn't my parents' fault that I had ended up on the streets. I made the decisions that got me there. That was *all* me.

Just like this was all *her*.

She had to take responsibility for her actions, just like I did.

All I could do was hold space for her when and if she was ever ready to choose life.

It was not and is still not my place to decide what is right for anyone, even my mom.

That is up to her. The only thing I have control over is who and what I allow into my life.

It took four days for the sedatives to filter through her system and allow her to open her eyes. But when she did, there was no response. Three days went by without following any prompts or showing any indication that she knew we were there. If this went on much longer, I knew they would put her back under again for observation. A part of me knew if they did that, I'd never get my mom back. I couldn't let that happen.

I stood next to my mom's bedside, grabbed her hand, and pleaded with her, just as I had the day before and the day before that.

"Mom, I know you're in there. I know it's hard and I know you're scared, but if you can hear me, let me know. Squeeze my hand or wiggle your toes or blink your eyes . . . something . . . anything!"

Then for the first time in almost four weeks, she blinked.

I almost couldn't believe it.

Actually, I didn't believe it, so I yelled to the nurse to come and asked my mom to do it again.

Then right in front of both of us, it happened again. My mom blinked on command.

She was there.

My mom was there.

I fell to the ground sobbing so heavily the nurse began fussing over me to make sure I was okay. I was more than okay—my mom knew I was there.

The next few weeks were non-stop work. I would give her a ChapStick to open, or a pen to practice writing and using her hands. We would practice our sounds as she learned to speak again when the tube from her tracheotomy was removed. We would do physical therapy in the bed between her real appointments with the physical therapist, and six weeks from the time she was admitted, she was home, healing and continuing to work on her recovery.

I am so proud to say that she has continued to work a program of whole-health recovery—mind, body, and spirit.

She is getting up and walking two miles every day, eating clean (for the most part), reading for pleasure again, finding things that bring her joy, building an amazing relationship with my dad (her husband of forty years), going on adventures, traveling the country, and is an incredible example of what it looks like to actively practice lifestyle recovery.

Her story is beautiful, but the truth is, it could have gone either way.

I often get asked, *What would you do if she relapsed?*

I tell them the same thing I told her.

I would make sure she was connected to another lifeline and I would let her go.

She knows what I went through by her side day and night.

She knows it is not something I would do a second time; not now that she is in her right mind and has a *choice*.

Yeah, you read that right.

She is *not* powerless. She is a fully grown woman capable of deciding if it's a good idea or not to take a drink.

If she picks up, it is absolutely a *choice*. One with real life consequences. She is well aware of my boundaries and respects them with love, one hundred percent.

Today, we have a relationship I never thought was possible.

I'm not telling you this story so that you run out and cut all ties with family and friends just because you don't like what they do.

I am telling you this story because I know what it's like to be taken down with the ship when it is sinking.

I know what it's like to love someone so much that you are willing to stand back and watch them kill themselves as you die slowly alongside them.

I'm telling you this story because I want you to know that you don't have to feel guilty for saving your own life. Whatever that looks like.

You deserve to honor what is right for you in your own life and you have the same right to decide what doesn't fit.

When we honor our 'yeses' and 'nos,' we align with who we are truly meant to be in this life.

Other people don't have to like it or be comfortable with it. The only person who has to experience the results is you.

PART FIVE

AUTHENTICITY

Chapter Twenty

GETTING HONEST

Who am I?

The ultimate question and by far the most complex.

In the early years of my recovery, after my first official arrest, I was ordered by the court to get sober or face jail time. I signed a deal for Prop 36, which gave me the chance to go to rehab instead of jail.

I was eighteen years old and had been using drugs since I was thirteen. I had been numbing myself for such a significant part of my life that I had no clue what the point of life was or how to deal with any of it. But I was desperate to learn.

I was directed by the courts into the rooms of Narcotics Anonymous (NA) and Alcoholics Anonymous (AA). They told me that if I kept my head down, did what they told me, got a sponsor, and worked these twelve steps that it would save my life.

So, I did.

But it didn't really work out like I had hoped.

What I had done was hand my life over to someone else and leave all the big decisions to them. I blindly followed the path I was being led down, not knowing anything other than that I had to do this to save my life. But all it did was teach me to follow the leader. I was still just as blind and disconnected from myself as ever.

They didn't know how to help me to learn what was right for *me* in *my* life.

Instead, what I got was some really bad examples and a lot of mixed signals.

The first two women who agreed to sponsor me never would return my calls. They told me to call every single day, so I did. But the only time I'd ever actually talk to them was at the meetings—if they showed up.

I found a new sponsor, one who actually answered my calls, and began working the steps.

She sponsored quite a few other women, so when I would see her at meetings, it was more like a social club or popularity contest than a meeting of AA.

As I'd sit there, listening to the speakers share about their journeys, my "sponsor" would be texting on her phone, gossiping about the speakers to others in the meeting, side-chatting, and full-on disrespecting those who were sharing.

This was my example? This is what I was looking up to?

What was I supposed to learn from this?

I knew I had to find another sponsor, but I had a difficult time connecting to the different cliques in the rooms.

It felt like high school all over again.

The box.

I was told repeatedly that if I wasn't doing what they wanted me to do, the way everyone else had done it, I would end up back on the streets or dead. That I didn't stand a chance.

But you know what I learned later that they didn't tell me then?

That if we live our life according to everyone else, we will never experience true personal freedom, and to me, that is a fate worse than death.

Some may consider just being clean from drugs freedom.

And it definitely was for me at first, but it didn't last long.

We call that the "pink cloud" syndrome. You are finally clear for the first time in years, if not decades, and you have a sense that anything is possible. It is, but life is still in session.

Fears, doubts, and uncomfortable emotions you have been numbing for as long as you can remember are going to come bubbling to the surface and can leave you wanting to crawl back under the rock you'd been hiding under for so long.

I did what I was told and managed to put together four years of clean time.

My first year, I went back to school, got my cosmetology license, and started my first business as a hairstylist.

Four years in, at twenty-two years old, I was four years sober, still going to meetings, working nonstop, malnourished from not taking care of myself, and in a terribly unhealthy relationship.

I had been discussing marriage with a man weeks before he relapsed on alcohol.

I'll never forget the moment I smelled it on his breath. My entire life flashed before my eyes as if it was already over. The enemy had already won.

What was going to happen to me now?

My codependency was at an all-time high in my life and I was scared of what it would look like alone. I didn't know what would happen, but I knew that the sobriety I was hanging onto for dear life wouldn't last long if I didn't make him leave.

He didn't go without a fight, but deep down, I knew I had to stand my ground. It took days of chaos and arguing, pleading, and tears to make him leave and convince him to stay gone.

But within just a few weeks, he was desperate to get back together, and to be honest, I was just as desperate to make everything go back to the way it was *before* the relapse.

I believed it was just his drinking that broke us up and I was determined to put everything back together with this idea of a life I *believed* we had before it all fell apart.

Funny how we seem to remember things the way we want to, isn't it?

I called around and found him a bed in a detox facility and supported him over the next twenty-one days as he regained his bearings and got back on his feet.

We were only back together for a few days before he broke the news.

There had been this girl . . . but it hadn't meant anything . . . he had just needed her to help him forget about me . . . and she was, well . . . she was pregnant.

Pregnant?

How could he?

Omg. He didn't know.

Not only was she pregnant, but what he did not know was that six months prior, I had miscarried *our* baby.

I hadn't shared this news with him because I didn't know how to.

I actually never told anyone until just a few years ago.

How could I? What would I say? I didn't even know how *I* felt about it. I didn't know I was pregnant until I miscarried my baby at ten weeks.

How do you process the realization that you had been growing a life inside of you, and at the same moment, process that you are losing that life?

I was devastated and confused. But at the same time, I was lost in guilt for being relieved.

How do you communicate that to anyone?

How do you even communicate that to yourself?

Though we had been talking about marriage, we were not in a good place. We didn't know how to talk to each other. Our friendship was long gone and we were just going through the motions because it was easier than facing the reality that we had no business being together anymore.

We fought every single day, rarely got along, and we would go days saying horrible things to each other out of spite, throwing things, and physically abusing each other.

But no one else knew that. At least we didn't think so. We kept that part to ourselves because wasn't that just part of being in a relationship? Taking the good with the bad? Everyone has their ups and downs, right? I've never met anyone who didn't fight and have arguments. We're all broken in some way and everyone always warns that the grass is never greener on the other side. So, I stayed. Who was I to think I deserved better? I was just a powerless addict, right? I still didn't know how to identify as anything else.

Marriage is just the next indicated step after being with someone for a few years, and that's what I had been instructed to do: take the next indicated step. I was being influenced from every direction that that was the "right" thing to do, and in the program, we followed directions, no matter how uncomfortable. It was our "responsibility."

Now, hearing that this woman was pregnant, it confirmed that I wasn't meant to bring a child into this world with that man.

In fact, that was my cue to get the heck out.

I packed a few things and left.

There was no passing go, no collecting two hundred dollars, just a trip straight to the dope dealer's house.

I didn't stand a chance. I couldn't feel this.

This couldn't be happening.

I had to escape the pain.

I knew how to do that.

Chapter Twenty-One

LIFESTYLE RECOVERY

When I was released from prison in 2010, after that final run, I knew I needed recovery so I reached out to the few people I still knew who were rocking their sobriety in the rooms of local anonymous programs.

The rooms of AA and NA really had impacted my life, so I wanted to implement them along this journey, but at the same time, I knew I needed more.

I went to a few meetings, but I kept getting that same old nagging feeling that there has to be more to life than mimicking the lives of others.

I tried not to judge, but when I was brutally honest with myself about what I was witnessing, I was not inspired.

While everyone may have been clean and sober, their lifestyle habits were still the same as if they had been using. They were still disconnecting from their feelings and looking for escapes, even if it wasn't with drugs and alcohol: five cups of coffee at 8:00 p.m., cupcakes, cookies, cigarettes, infidelity, gossip, trash talk, constant judgment. They were all still completely disconnected from themselves and their own well-being.

I had to get honest with myself about whether or not I really wanted what they had.

One Friday night, at one of the last meetings I have ever attended, an older gentleman stood up to share. I watched him slowly make his way up to the podium, heavy with the weight of his pain and sadness.

He shared that he had over twenty-three years of continuous sobriety and that his life still sucked.

That it was hard and if we expected it to get easier just because we were sober, we were wrong. He went on for ten minutes talking about all of the struggles in his life. That there is no such thing as personal freedom and that no matter how much work you do, life will always be hard.

I understood what he meant. That life is always going to throw challenges your way, but I didn't believe that we were always meant to struggle. I believed there was a way to real, lasting freedom.

I knew that he was just one man and that I shouldn't lump everyone in the room into his way of thinking, but there was a trend.

I looked around the room.

How many of these people were truly free?

How many of them knew all of their likes and dislikes? Their joy and their fears? Their purpose in life?

How many of these men and women actually took care of themselves instead of everyone else? How many knew who they were without someone telling them? How many knew how to be comfortable in their own skin? How many knew what *they* wanted or what *they* needed to be happy? How many knew how to set boundaries and heal their codependency?

I knew there were definitely successful people in the program, but I realized pretty quickly, I wanted more.

I didn't just *want* more, I *needed* more. I needed whole-health recovery. I needed *lifestyle recovery*.

I didn't want to live in fear and scarcity. I wanted to learn how to live in faith and abundance.

I needed to learn to trust myself. I needed to learn how to connect to my current experience and be okay in my own skin, without feeling the need to escape or distract myself.

I needed to learn how to take inspired action towards my goals, instead of fear-based action. I needed to find a healthy balance with family, friends, work, fun, health, and a career I love.

I needed to be able to go anywhere and do anything without needing to identify as an addict or an alcoholic every time I made a decision.

If I couldn't identify as anything besides a powerless addict, how could I become anything else?

I needed to be able to be honest with anyone and everyone when they asked my opinion, even if they didn't agree. I needed to be able to say 'no' to the things that no longer served me, no matter how uncomfortable it was.

So, I started to pay attention. Especially when it came down to honoring what I needed from myself.

When I needed to rest, I rested. When I needed to get rid of built-up anxiety, I went for a walk or run, or if it was really bad, I'd lift weights. When I was hungry, I ate. Even if it wasn't the most convenient time. I even started to pay attention to *how* I ate. Not just the types of food, but the actual way I was eating my meals.

Was I actually present when I was eating? Tasting, smelling, and experiencing the meal?

Or was I rushing to my next appointment, driving, watching TV, or otherwise distracted?

When I did start to pay attention, I also began to notice which foods made me feel good and which ones made me feel like crap. When I was honest with myself about which foods my body liked and which ones it didn't, the decisions started to make themselves.

My mind and body would connect and align, and when I would start to go for foods that didn't serve me—meaning they gave me digestive upset, a foggy brain, or a headache—I would instinctively choose differently.

When I became anxious (the trigger for my emotional eating), I would simply go outside to take some deep, long breaths of fresh air or go for a walk.

Taking care of myself just started to make more sense. It began to become part of who I was.

When I was honest about what I was experiencing, I was then able to make small shifts to enhance that experience.

I started to have more meaningful conversations with the people in my life and learned who I was in alignment with and who I wasn't. Without judgment, I slowly started removing myself from the situations that were more of a distraction than a support.

I began to notice a crazy amount of resistance that came up every time I attempted to be honest about wanting to stay in or declining invitations to meetings and other events.

I would get tense and sick with guilt. So, I would sit with the tension for a moment to feel into it.

What was I so scared of?

Will they be upset with me for saying 'no'?

Will they stop calling me? Or caring about me?

Will they speak badly about me to others? Will they think I'm selfish?

It took a while to get comfortable with what I am about to tell you, but I learned how to say this one little thing, with so much clarity, power, and authority that the guilt has subsided, and I have been able to be an example of what it looks like to create an authentic, abundant life and career of serving others.

Want to know what that word is?

'No.'

That's it! It's that simple. One word, one meaning, and the same in most languages.

The best part is that you don't even have to explain yourself.

You can, of course, politely decline with something like, "Sounds like it's gonna be a blast, but I'm not going to be able to make it. I hope you have so much fun!"

Or, "Thank you so much for thinking of me! Unfortunately, I won't be able to make it, but I appreciate the invitation!"

But you don't *owe* anyone an explanation for why you will or won't do something.

When you honor your boundaries *authentically*, you are honoring more than just yourself. You are also honoring those who love you by giving them the most genuine, fully embodied version of yourself. You inevitably realize that it is better for *everyone* when you are mentally, emotionally, and physically healthy. The guilt of saying 'no' can't help but lose its grip on you when you are coming from a loving, authentic place.

When you show up with your tank empty, or as only a partial version of yourself, you deny the people closest to you the honor of actually knowing and loving all of you. You allow room for self-doubt and a fear to creep in that one day they may get to know the real you and not love you anymore.

When you put all your cards on the table, you reveal the most authentic version of yourself and only then will you fully align with who you were meant to be in this life.

It takes courage to put every part of yourself out there. Being vulnerable is not for the weak. According to Brené Brown in *The Gifts of Imperfection*, being your authentic self is a conscious and courageous choice.

Pause and Reflect

Taking courageous action can sometimes exhaust us on a level we aren't familiar with. When you are a newly recovering codependent, setting authentic boundaries for the first time can sometimes even feel physically painful. You may get the chills or get cramps in your stomach. You might even get a headache or stiffness in your neck.

Try one (or a few) of these simple tricks that have saved me from collapsing after my early attempts to set new boundaries and honor my needs ahead of others:

Take deep breaths and ground into your current experience. Notice what is coming up for you and allow the feelings or thoughts to just be there. Then remind yourself (and all of your parts) that you are safe and loved and that you are of better service to everyone when you are fully sourced.

Listen to an inspirational podcast or audio book.

Stand in front of the mirror and thank the person looking back at you for standing up for what you need and deserve in your life.

Go for a walk around the block and remind yourself why taking care of your own health, happiness, and well-being is actually beneficial to everyone you care about because you can show up for them as your best self.

Chapter Twenty-Two

I AM

For years in the program, I had been told over and over that I was powerless. I repeated it so much that I actually believed it.

While I can admit powerlessness over other people, places, and things, I am *far* from powerless in deciding what my experience is going to be in this life.

I have the power to change my experience at any given time.

"I am" is one of, if not *the* most powerful statements in the human language.

That *is* power. That is manifestation.

The words you speak to yourself and out loud into the world hold power.

Every single day we are deciding who we are.

The problem is, when we are making that decision, we are being influenced by more than we realize.

Your parents, your friends, your colleagues, teachers, television, social media, movies, music, and your environment are all influencing who you decide to be, every moment of every day. It's no wonder so many of us struggle with our identity.

Every single client I have mentioned so far in my book, including my own mom, all suffered from a lack of identity and a broken belief system.

They believed certain things were true about the world and identified a certain way as a result of those beliefs.

Have you ever heard the quote from Henry Ford, "Whether you think you can or you think you can't, you're right"?

It speaks more to belief than anything. When we believe something is true, we look for evidence to prove it.

If we believe we don't have time, we will look at all of the things we have to do and how busy we are.

If we believe we don't have what it takes to start a business, we will look at all the examples of why it just wouldn't work: too much time, too much money, too unstable and risky. . . .

If we believe our genetics won't allow us to be healthy, we will never seek answers for our own health and wellness. Instead we resolve ourselves to living an unhealthy lifestyle because, *What's the point of trying?*

If we believe we will fail just because we don't do exactly what one person or one group tells us, we will never trust that we know what is right for ourselves. We will always question our choices and never truly learn to trust our own decisions.

Conversely, if we believe that we *can* be successful, we begin to look for proof of that conviction. If we believe we have time to work out or prepare healthy meals, we will find the time. If we believe we can start a thriving business, we will take the steps required to make it happen. If we believe in our own power, we will make choices that serve our authentic selves. It is up to us to decide what we believe is true.

Pause and Reflect

Connect into your current experience. Does it feel aligned with your goals? How does it affect your balance? Will it break any boundaries you have set up for yourself? Does this support the very best version of you and the life you want?

If so, lean in and trust that you are making the best decision you can for yourself now, at this moment.

If not, let it go with love, knowing what is meant for you will show itself as long as you stay true to yourself.

It was March of 2020 and the entire world was on lockdown because of the COVID-19 pandemic.

People were scared to leave their homes and were actually encouraged not to. Fear, uncertainty, and anxiety swept the globe. Families, friends, and entire communities were scared, confused, completely unsure of what to do, and many began turning on each other.

It honestly made me sick to see the way people were behaving towards one another. People I *knew*. Parents were turning on their adult children. Siblings and former best friends were wishing death on each other, either for being vaccinated or not being vaccinated. Wearing masks or not wearing masks. Challenging the system or not challenging the system. Both sides were willing to die for their beliefs, convinced the other side was the problem.

Toss in a year of social isolation, disrupted work, economic instability, and broken family routines, and the fear, isolation, and powerlessness led to all-out emotional chaos.

People were so chronically disconnected from themselves that they had completely lost touch with who they were being.

I sat back and watched it all like a bad car accident you can't help but slow down to see.

I could see why each side had their stance and I found myself somewhere in between. I am a person who believes in evidence-based science and what is true for me, based on my own personal experience—not just the opinions of others.

As a functional health coach, transformational life coach, and certified personal trainer, I've studied functional nutrition for years. I knew well the importance of a healthy gut biome, the way different systems work in our body, the effects that proper nutrition, exercise, and lifestyle habits have on our health, and because of this, at no point was I scared of getting sick or of consequently dying from this virus. I knew that I had done everything in my power to support my body in having a solid immune system and that my body had an amazing chance at fighting this thing off.

But when it came to my parents or loved ones with chronic illnesses, I absolutely believed that they needed extra support with their immune system.

What killed me was the fact that the American government missed a huge opportunity to teach people how to *actually* take care of themselves.

They *forgot* to mention that sugar feeds inflammation and that it was an inflammatory virus.

They forgot to mention that exercise, balanced meals with whole foods, and good sleep help build our bodies' defenses against illness. In fact, they closed our gyms.

They *forgot* to mention that loneliness causes depression, and we lose almost fifty thousand people per year to suicide. Instead, they told us not to spend holidays with our families or gather with friends.

The entire world was completely shut down and everything we knew before was gone.

No one really understood what was happening, and as panic set in, the world fell into crisis. I don't know one person who didn't lose someone they cared about to COVID-19. Not just to the illness itself, but the consequences of the lockdown.

Hospitals everywhere were flooded beyond capacity. Stretchers lined the hallways, patients were lying on the floors of the waiting rooms, waiting hours on end to be seen. There were constant shortages of nurses, hospital staff, and overwhelmed first responders, as well as riots in the otherwise empty streets. Buildings were burning, people were dying, and it felt like the end of the world to so many.

While I was definitely scared of the unknown, what I did know was that I had been through worse. I had been in real prison—both mentally and physically. I knew how to find freedom within myself, so when my freedom to live my life *outside* was threatened, I was still okay. I had learned how to shift my state of being in *any* situation. I had learned how to choose my experience, even when the world was falling apart around me.

I knew that the universe had brought me this far, and if it wanted to take me out with this virus, so be it.

All I could do was show up for myself, even if the world shut down around me.

There is an innate sense of power and personal freedom we uncover when we learn to shift who we are being in any given moment or circumstance.

You are the creator of your experience. When you learn to master this, you learn to master your life.

Chapter Twenty-Three

PARTS WORK

2019

Being honest with ourselves and living authentically is one of the most difficult parts of lifestyle recovery. The weight of realizing that *we* are the reason we are where we are in life can be heavy to carry at first.

Once you begin to work the steps of the freedom framework, the load starts to lighten and you begin to experience what true personal freedom feels like: the ability to live an abundant, authentic life, unfettered by the opinions of others, following your dreams, supporting what you believe in, and allowing others to do the same.

The moment I realized my personal salvation had nothing to do with everyone else, and everything to do with who I was being, my life changed.

I'd love to say, "Now I know who I am and everything is so easy," but I'd be lying.

The truth is, when my coaching practice began to do well and gain traction, all the different parts of me that I thought I had healed started to compete for attention: the part of me that's a know-it-all, the drop-out, the mental patient, the homeless teen, the convicted felon, the co-dependent. . . . They were all there, rearing their ugly heads, causing the most crippling cases of imposter syndrome I had ever experienced. None of them believed in who I claimed to be.

What the hell?

I thought I had dealt with all of this?!

Guess not.

It was time to follow my own advice, get curious, and do some deeper work.

I turned off my phone and sat down at my dining room table.

This was the first time I had ever tried this exercise myself, outside of working with a coach or delivering it during a client session. I wasn't sure how it was going to go, but I had to try it. I felt so stuck. My mind was cluttered with self-doubt and old stories, and I had to get it all out on the table if I was going to have any success at reaching my goals.

I closed my eyes and set my intentions for this experience. I wanted to get clear on what was coming up for each of my parts, so I invited them all to the table.

I imagined in my mind's eye, all of the different parts of me, there, in the room, at the dining room table.

The three-year-old part of me who was ignorantly blissful to the real world and just wanted everyone to be happy.

The twelve-year-old part of me who was lost and overwhelmed and bored all at the same time and just wanted everyone to like her.

The seventeen-year-old who was homeless, severely mentally ill, sticking needles in her arms to get loaded and escape any sense of reality.

The twenty-year-old who had a few years clean and had all the answers.

The twenty-two-year-old who relapsed and ended up back on the streets, losing all faith in herself.

The twenty-five-year-old who was in prison for the second time, desperate to make a change and save her own life.

The twenty-eight-year-old who weighed all her food and walked around at 7 percent body fat.

They were all there and they *all* had something to say.

Talk about a weird-ass family reunion.

Just like at every one of our Italian family dinners, every part was speaking over each other, getting louder and louder to dominate the conversation.

Each part believed they had more authority than the other and it was utter chaos.

Seventeen-year-old Jenn said, "Fuck this, you know you're just going to go back to getting loaded, why make all this effort?"

Twenty-five-year-old said, "Don't say that! We have to try!"

Twelve-year-old said, "We don't know that, maybe we should ask someone else's opinion?"

Twenty-two-year-old said, "You can't rely on anyone else, why would you ask them?"

Twenty-year-old said, "You just need to give people a chance; they may surprise you."

Seventeen-year-old said, "You can't trust anyone. You might as well just give up!"

Twenty-eight-year-old said, "It doesn't matter how you feel just do it anyway."

The present version of me couldn't take it anymore. I was done being torn apart by all my different beliefs and identities. Without another second of hesitation, I took command of the "meeting." I began to sit with each part and listen. I checked in on their intentions, and nine times out of ten, they were all just trying to keep me safe. Safe from failing as a coach, as an author, as a daughter, as a friend, as a human being.

I connected to and held space for each part to be seen and heard. Even the parts . . . *especially* the parts that were the most afraid.

I realized that each part had developed a different way of coping with life. Each of them was scared by the potential of history repeating itself. But they were all relying on *old data*.

I wasn't who I used to be, or around the people and situations I used to be.

I spoke up firmly and clearly, asserting my position as the CEO of my own life. "I appreciate all you have done to keep me safe. I know each of you have your own reasons for keeping me from moving forward, but I am ready to try something different. I am going to trust that this present version of me is capable of anything I set my mind to. I know that everything we have done to get to this place in life has prepared me for where I am going and who I will become. I am resilient. I am a different kind of strong."

I had to build a healthy relationship of trust and communication with *myself* and all of my parts before I was ever going to be capable of sharing the most authentic version of myself with others.

Pause and Reflect

True personal freedom comes from authenticity: our ability to be honest with ourselves and others no matter what.

What parts of you are you afraid to show to the world?

Are you being honest with yourself about what you really want?

Are you playing small to make others feel safe?

What would it take for you to lead a fully authentic life?

PART SIX

ACCOUNTABILITY

Chapter Twenty-Four

WHO ARE YOU BEING?

Accountability: "The obligation or willingness to accept responsibility for one's actions."

Woah.

Now, hold on now a sec there, Webster. That's a little heavy!

Not sure why, but when I read that dictionary definition for the first time, a thousand-pound weight settled over me that made me struggle to breathe.

I knew better than the next guy how important it was for me to take responsibility for my actions. To apologize when I was wrong and face the consequences.

But that was when I'd wronged others.

That was when someone was in my face telling me I did something wrong.

Damn, there it was. The missing piece. All bright and shiny, printed in black on the dusty white pages of the three-inch hardback *Webster's* dictionary in the prison library.

I had never actually been held accountable for anything in my entire life.

I was an only child and my daddy's little girl. Even when I was shooting methamphetamine straight into my veins and stealing anything that wasn't nailed down to get my next fix, according to him, it had to be someone else's fault.

When I wasn't showing up to school because I was too busy getting high at friends' houses, my dad actually showed up to one of the houses with a baseball bat, threatening to beat them down if they didn't send me out. He believed it was their fault I was ditching school and getting loaded.

I wasn't actually there at the time, or they would have handed me over in a heartbeat. No one wants to mess with a pissed off parent.

Especially one with a bat.

When I was eighteen and working my first twelve-step program, I had to create an inventory of all of the significant events that I've experienced in my life and how they still affected me to that day. What I started to put together was that I had no real discipline or authority in my childhood, and instead of taking responsibility for being an asshole, I blamed my parents for my lack of direction and self-control.

I blamed the school system for not paying enough attention to me.

I blamed the guys I had dated for my trust issues.

The system for failing us all.

It wasn't until I stood in front of the judge yet again, facing six years in state prison, that I learned what accountability really even meant.

Until then, none of it really mattered. None of the consequences in my past ever really stuck. They were all just another reason to blame the system and everyone else. But this time, it wasn't just a slap on the wrists.

This time the consequences meant long, hard time upstate.

Time to press pause and take a serious look at the life I had been living and the choices I had been making that led me to that courtroom with a rap sheet with the makings of a career criminal.

Talk about being scared. I was about to learn what accountability *really* looked like.

I was *not* excited.

I stood in front of the judge at the Riverside Superior Courthouse. He wasn't a large man, by any means, but his presence and power flooded the courtroom. I had never really accepted full responsibility for my actions before, but here I was, standing in that courtroom, admitting guilt. It wasn't the first time I had stood in front of the judge, or the first time I was found guilty, but this was different. This time I was choosing to fully accept accountability for my actions.

By that point, I had been arrested more times than I could count. I had even already served one prison term, but obviously it still hadn't been enough to get me to stop. I had broken too many laws for too many years and it was time to face the consequences. I was looking at six years if I was sent to trial, so I was there to make a plea deal and settle for an eighteen-month sentence.

The shame I felt was indescribable. It filled my entire being, making me feel so small I didn't know how the judge could still see me standing there.

"Ms. Henry, how do you plead?"

I tried to speak up, but the words caught in my throat like a dry piece of chicken. My brain attempted to process what was happening. I had to admit guilt and admitting guilt meant prison. But denying guilt meant I got to spend the next year fighting my case from county jail. If I lost, I could get six years instead of eighteen months, and let's face it, I was guilty.

So, with every ounce of strength and self-discipline I could muster, I responded with a broken, shaky voice, "Guilty, your Honor."

He accepted my guilty plea and I was ushered back to the cold, wet holding cell below the courthouse.

Once I was back in the cell, the guard unchained my wrists from my waist and handed me my paper sack lunch. I sat down, deciding on the bruised apple over the dry bologna and cheese sandwich it had been paired with.

What had just happened? I had always defended myself. I had always had some reason, some excuse why it wasn't really my fault. Why I was just in the wrong place at the wrong time or some sob story about not knowing what I was doing because I was loaded.

This time was different. I had to face reality. I had to be honest with myself about who I was being. This time there was no out. This time I was facing the consequences head on.

Then I learned my lesson and I never did anything wrong ever again.

Ha! Right. Like that's how it works.

Wouldn't that be nice though? If one day we just woke up and decided to be different and we developed healthy habits and started to take care of ourselves, and situations in life just got easier?

While it doesn't just happen at the snap of a finger, the truth is that all it really takes is a little bit of accountability.

Taking responsibility for who you are being at any given moment, *regardless* of the circumstances.

I'm going to say it louder for the people in the back: *You are responsible for who you are being at any given moment, regardless of the circumstances.*

When it comes down to it, we are all accountable on some level to someone or something.

Is it your boss? The time you have to clock in? Customers, patients, or clients you serve? Your spouse or children? Friends? Your parents? Mortgage company? Your HOA? A teacher?

A coach? God? Mohammed? Jesus? Gandhi? Santa?

We show up for all of these other commitments in our lives without hesitation, being held to a certain level of accountability. A certain standard.

But what standards are you holding yourself accountable to in your own life?

Pause and Reflect

*What are the standards you have set up
for your health?*

*Is your baseline daily movement or no movement?
Balanced meals? Or a bag of chips for lunch?*

What are the standards in your relationships?

*Do you demand open communication? Loyalty?
Trust? Or do you accept anything in order
not to be alone?*

What is your standard for your finances?

*Do you make sure you don't spend more than you
make? Or do you keep spending as long as there's
room on the credit card?*

Your standards are the foundation of your life experience. It is up to you to set the standards you want to live by and hold yourself accountable to them.

May 2011

I had been out of rehab for four weeks and I had gone for a run every single day. The habits I had started in New Hope carried over into my everyday life at home. In the beginning, it was all I needed. The feeling of freedom as I pushed my body past what I believed it was capable of. But after just a few weeks, it didn't matter how long or how far I ran, it didn't feel like enough. I felt like I needed something more, so I went online to learn how to lift weights. I signed up for a free program on bodybuilding.com, got myself a gym membership, and got to work.

Every day after work, I'd head straight to the gym. Right there in the weight room, I would open the app on my phone, watch the videos, and copy the form as best I could.

Yes, right in front of everybody.

I know. Crazy, right?

I was honestly scared shitless of making a fool of myself, but if I can stand up to a bunch of convicted felons over a treadmill, I can stand up to a bunch of jocks, right?

Well, that's what I had to tell myself to get my ass in that gym.

I won't lie. I sat in that parking lot for quite a while before I went in. I wasn't sure exactly what I was really hoping to get out of all this, but I sure as hell wasn't going to figure it out sitting in the damn parking lot.

The more I showed up, the easier it got to park and walk inside.

The more I showed up, the more I learned to trust myself. The more I trusted myself, the safer I felt to push myself in every area of my life. The more I pushed myself, the better I became at dealing with my own stubborn resistance.

Before long, I realized I wasn't just building my muscles or lifting weights, I was holding myself to new standards. To a new level of accountability. I was becoming a different kind of strong.

In order to keep growing, my level of accountability had to continue to grow as well.

I was setting solid standards for myself in my life, but if I wanted to grow, I needed to set some goals too.

Purposeful daily movement was my standard. It was my non-negotiable.

But my goal was now to see what my body was truly capable of when I doubled down on my health and fitness. I wanted to learn how to sculpt my body and compete on stage.

Over the next few years, I became certified as a personal trainer and began training others while I was training for my own shows. I held myself accountable, studied hard, and put in the work.

I loved every part of prepping for competition. The early morning cardio and the late-night workouts, the pre-planned meals I didn't even have to think about. The structure and routine was so new to me, and I had no idea how incredibly freeing having a routine could really be.

I wasn't just waking up and letting the day unfold where it may, I was setting specific intentions and making decisions about how I was going to spend my time and energy.

But I knew that if I really wanted to get to the next level, I needed more support and guidance. I needed someone to help hold the vision for me from an outside perspective.

I'll never forget the resistance I felt around hiring my first nutrition coach for a fitness competition I was planning on entering.

2014

Having coached myself all the way to the stage for the first five competitions already, I wasn't 100 percent convinced I really needed anyone else's help. I had taken home three wins of the five shows I'd competed in and was pretty pleased with the results. The problem was I had never competed in this particular federation before and it was a completely different format.

I knew that if I wanted to show up and be taken seriously, I needed some guidance.

Reluctantly, I reached out to a well-known professional coach in the federation and asked him if he was willing to coach an amateur client, who had never competed in their federation before.

To my surprise, he said 'yes' and we got to work.

The fact that someone like him, who worked with professional athletes all over the world, said 'yes' to working with me, lit something inside of me that I didn't even know was there.

I realized I wasn't fighting for my life anymore. A part of me was ready to fight for my dreams.

I was fighting to be seen and heard. I was fighting to take up space. I was fighting to show my value and worth. I was fighting to show up as my best self in this life.

Over the following ten weeks, I worked harder than I ever had before. I honestly believed that I had set high standards for myself in the gym and in the kitchen. It wasn't until I hired that coach that I actually realized how impactful the accountability of having another set of eyes and ears really is.

We are at average 65 percent more likely to reach our goals just by simply making a commitment to someone else. Those odds increase significantly when you actually invest in a coach or mentor. Every single one of us is stronger when we are supported in our journeys.

I learned more about body composition in those ten weeks than I had in three years of certifications and self-study. I didn't take home the win, but I looked and felt better than I had at any other show I'd competed in before then.

I realized that no matter what I wanted to accomplish, if I wanted to find out what I was truly capable of, I needed someone who was at least one step ahead of me to show me what that could look like. I needed guidance and support. Not someone who would do the work for me, but someone who I respected enough to actually hold *myself* accountable to.

Years later, my first business coach, Christine Williams, said to me, "You can't read the label from inside the bottle."

I had been struggling to build my coaching business online and I knew I needed another set of eyes on my goals to help give me a clearer vision of what was truly possible. She was the first person who actually held the vision with me that I was capable of making six figures doing what I love.

Accountability is a practice. Even if I pay tens of thousands of dollars for a coach or mentor or support community, if I don't have some level of self-accountability, the money won't matter. Making a significant investment in a coach or to be a part of a mastermind helps to hold my ass to the fire, but when it comes down to it, I still have to show up! The more we show up, the more we begin to trust ourselves again. The more we trust, the more we begin to believe in ourselves and what we are capable of.

Chapter Twenty-Five

LEVELING UP

The level of accountability I have invested in has shifted many times over the years.

It started in 2010 with the mandatory weekly drug tests and check-ins with my parole officer for eighteen months post-release. This was pretty much forced accountability, and while I hated every second of it, it is what taught me to show up whether I liked it or not.

Over the course of that year and a half, my parole officer changed four times. Every single time I had to reintroduce myself, the new officer would judge me and make assumptions that I was just like every other parolee they've ever had to deal with. That meant every single time, I had to prove myself all over again. As much as I hated that cycle, I found that I *loved* to prove them wrong. I was *not* going to be a statistic. I wasn't going to follow the status quo. I was going to learn to hold myself accountable, whether the State of California was involved in my life or not.

(In fact, I need to thank the California government that was in place back in 2010 because if it wasn't for getting arrested and getting assigned the support and accountability I desperately needed at the time, I guarantee you I wouldn't be here to tell you these stories.

My hope is that we can build a state government that actually cares about those of us who don't know how to care about ourselves.)

Over the last ten years, I have invested more than a hundred thousand dollars in coaches and masterminds. I've been without a coach during periods of my life, but when I look back to those times, I can see how easily I was derailed. I have the best of intentions, but I haven't always had the best strategies. By investing in coaching and mentorship, I have not only been taught the right strategies, but now I also have the support to consistently follow through and stay in alignment with my goals.

Whether it was a parole officer assigned through the state or whether I invested tens of thousands of dollars in a coaching program, both extremes taught me that if I want the best results, I have to show up for *myself*.

I didn't *have* to check in with my parole officer, but if I didn't, I was going back to prison.

I don't *have* to show up to my mastermind calls, but if I don't, I won't be inspired by or benefit from the depth of knowledge and wisdom all of the other women in the group possess.

I don't *have* to go to the gym, but if I don't, my depression will kick in and I won't get anything done for days, which will only fuel my depression more.

I don't *have* to sleep six hours minimum, but if I don't, I'm a worthless zombie all day.

I don't *have* to have a morning routine, but if I don't, my day falls apart before it even starts.

Are you getting the point?

We don't *have* to do *anything*.

So, no matter what tools I use to support myself in showing up, I still have to make the choice to actually show up for myself or not.

There are so many ways to hold yourself accountable. Choosing what works best for you is going to be key in your success.

Here are five ways Tony Robbins suggests to uplevel your accountability:

1. Examine your beliefs and values.

Values are the basic foundation of our behavior, attitudes, and perceptions. We always make decisions about right and wrong based on our personal values.

If we value honesty, integrity, courage, loyalty, respect, and compassion, we show up differently in the world than if our values align with judgment, criticism, or fear.

Beliefs are what we accept to be true, even if we don't actually have any proof. They stem from our environment and past experiences, even if they were not our own. We are influenced by what we read, watch, and listen to, as well as who we are raised by and surround ourselves with throughout our lives.

What values do you live by? What is the standard you set for yourself?
What do you believe is true about the world?
What do you believe you are capable of?
What do you believe you deserve?

Maybe take a few minutes to journal and answer these questions for yourself.

2. Turn your "shoulds" into "musts."

Stop "shoulding" all over yourself! "Should" according to whom? This is *your* life.

Stop telling yourself what you "should" be doing and start deciding what you *must* do.

When you set a goal, dig deep and ask yourself why it's so important to you. Tie it to your life's mission and make it non-negotiable. When you start to waiver, dig in and remind yourself *why* it is a must and why you absolutely will take action.

As Tony says, "If you can't, you must. If you must, you can."

3. Develop time management skills.

Being accountable can be tough when you feel like you don't have enough time in the day. But when you say, "I don't have time," what you're really saying is, "I don't know how to manage my time." Grab that to-do list and use time blocking to plan your day. Learn to use your time more efficiently. These are the small tasks that add up to a lot of wasted time in your day, like commuting and house cleaning, so use that time to listen to an audio book or podcast that feeds your mind and supports you in moving closer to your goals.

4. Mind your words.

Every single one of us has an inner monologue that affects the way we interact with the world. That little voice turns into the way we act and the words we speak. The ability to identify and shift any negative self-talk is vital to healthy relationships. Next time something doesn't go as planned, notice how you react. Is your "inner critic" blaming something other than yourself? Flip those thoughts around and think about how you can improve in the future. That's personal accountability.

5. Get support.

Having someone else who can hold you accountable can actually be the first step to developing personal accountability. Many of the most successful people will tell you they didn't do it alone. With the help of accountability coaching, you'll make a plan, set goals, and unlock your potential. Once you see the incredible things you can achieve, you'll be addicted to self-accountability.

I would love to believe that I am so accountable to my goals and dreams that I would show up even if I didn't make an investment, or even if my freedom wasn't on the line, but it's just simply not the case.

It's totally possible that I could have written this book on my own, without the support of my editor Audrey, my coach Sara, my publisher Patti, or my amazing and supportive community of other female authors and movement leaders.

Do I believe I would have actually finished it and gotten it published?

Not a chance.

Writing this book challenged me in ways I didn't even know were possible. I had made the decision to commit and make it happen, yet my gremlins, or inner critics, insisted I wasn't educated enough, didn't have the follow-through, and wasn't going to be taken seriously as an author or expert in my field.

I could have easily listened to them and doubted myself right into not following through. I could have decided that my subconscious was just trying to keep me safe, trusted that without question, and just kept playing small.

But instead, I doubled down.

Working with my coach, Christine, not only helped me to see that it was my responsibility to get my work out in the world, but that I was doing a disservice to those who needed my support and could not find me.

She called me out for playing small and constantly comparing myself against other successful people: "If they can do it, so can you, Jenn. Stop comparing yourself and start collaborating."

As part of her program, Christine would collaborate with other experts in our industry and bring them in as guest experts during our sessions to guide and support us in our different journeys as coaches and business owners. Watching her do this made me believe that I could too.

You know the saying, "When the student is ready, the teacher will appear"?

Over the years, I have had *countless* people tell me to write a book.

"OMG, you have to tell your story! It will impact so many lives!"

"Jenn, when are you going to write your book?"

"Jenn, you have to get your story out there!"

I'd just laugh it off and say, "Yeah that's a great idea, want to write it for me?"

Or, "When you find someone who will take over running my life for me while I write it, I'll do it."

I never really believed it was something I could ever do myself.

. . .

And then one day during one of my group sessions with Christine, there she was: Sara Connell.

The woman who was turning writing into a full-blown movement. She was the queen when it came to bestselling books and supporting other women in becoming bestselling authors and starting their own movements.

Even on Zoom, through the computer screen, Sara was a force of nature. She wasn't loud or aggressive, but she carried this beautiful quiet strength. The confidence of someone who knew who she was and what she was put on this planet to do.

I knew this wasn't a coincidence.

This wasn't my first connection to Sara. I had met with her two years prior, to discuss what it would look like to work with her to write my book. But at the time, I really didn't have the entire story. I hadn't built a six-figure business. In fact, I was still struggling to decide exactly *why* I really wanted to write the book.

I had the questions but not all the answers.

I knew I still had some work to do. I needed to test my framework and have the evidence to back it up.

Here we were, two years later, and I had found my niche, built my business, and knew I had a worthwhile story to share.

My framework was transforming lives and I wanted to tell the world about it.

"If they can do it, so can you, Jenn." Christine's words reverberated in my ears as I sat on a call with Sara, trying not to be intimidated by this powerhouse of a woman.

I don't even remember what Sara said the entire class. All I remember was that I was *in*.

It was a large investment and I didn't have the money, but based on my past experiences, I knew if it was meant to be part of my path, even if I couldn't see a way at first, one would always appear.

Because of the work I had done the last eleven years, I knew that what was meant for me would find me as long as I was connected and aligned to my purpose in this life.

I was meant to lead a movement. I was meant to play big, even if it makes others uncomfortable—even if it makes *me* uncomfortable.

I am not here to people-please and support people in their comfort zones.

I am here to shake shit up and be a force of nature. I am here to challenge everything you think you know about yourself and this world.

You weren't put on this earth to be ordinary. You were put on this earth to make a difference in people's lives. If you weren't, you wouldn't be reading this book.

If you weren't, you wouldn't be on this journey to personal growth or self-discovery.

You wouldn't be so uncomfortable with the status quo or the box they keep trying to squeeze you into. You wouldn't be questioning the decisions that have landed you where you are at this very moment.

But you need to know this: You, without a doubt, are exactly where you are supposed to be right now.

It is in this moment that you are meant to discover your truth.

Who and what are you holding yourself accountable to?

Who are you holding yourself accountable to being?

What are your standards?

What are your goals? Wants? Dreams? Desires?

Taking accountability for your life and the decisions that got you here is the only way to really decide what is meant for you and what isn't.

None of them were wrong. They were all made with the best of intentions. But remember, having good intentions is different than having a good strategy.

Starting today, pay attention. Ask yourself if the actions you are taking are in alignment with the life you want. Figure out where you are expending the most energy and make sure you have something set up to replace what you deplete. Say 'yes' to the things that serve you and keep you aligned and say 'no' to what pulls you off of your path.

Be honest with yourself and others about what you really need and find a way to hold yourself accountable. Find someone who will hold space for you to be your highest, most authentic self. Someone who allows you to make mistakes without judgment and holds your hand until you figure it out.

A coach, mentor, teacher, or counselor, someone who isn't your bestie or your mom. Someone who can call you out when you start to fall off track, without making you feel resentment towards them.

Accountability buddies are great, but if one falls off, it is more than likely the other will as well. When we invest in accountability, we aren't investing in the coach or mentor, we are investing in ourselves. We are investing in who we are capable of being and investing in someone to hold that vision for us.

From mindset, to business strategy, to writing, I have continued to invest in coaching year after year because it *works*.

People often ask how I did it.

"How did you go from being homeless to owning your own home free and clear, running two businesses, and having such a beautiful life?"

Simple.

Coaching. Support. Accountability.

That's how.

Did I have the money at first? *Nope!*

Did investing in a coach change that? *Yep!*

Why? Because someone was literally holding my hand as I created what I wanted.

Could I have done it by myself? Maybe.

Would I have? *Nope!*

I wish I could say that I am so good at holding myself accountable that I only needed to invest for my first few years in business and now I am good-to-go.

But that's simply just not the case. The truth is, not only do I *need* the support of my coaches and their communities, but I *want* it. I want to be a part of something bigger. I want to cheer on my brothers and sisters in starting their movements, just like they support me in mine.

As a coach, I will never be without a coach. Why would I ask someone to invest in something I myself am not investing in? I would be completely out of alignment and out of integrity.

If you are a personal trainer and you don't work out, I'm not going to hire you.

If you are a travel agent but have never been outside of your hometown. . . .

If you are trying to sell me followers on Instagram, but you only have 1200 followers. . . .

If you are trying to give me relationship advice but have never been in a long-term relationship. . . .

If you want to be my addictions counselor but have never used drugs or abused alcohol. . . .

Even if you have all the best training in the world. . . .

They are all going to be a 'no' from me.

Why?

Integrity. It's that simple.

I want to know you have walked the walk, not just learned how to talk the talk.

I want to know you have the experience, not just the knowledge. I want to know that you are a product of the work you do.

I talk the talk, but I also walk the walk.

Do you? Do the people you take advice from?

Are you surrounding yourself with people who are creating the kind of life you want to have? Or are you hanging out with what's familiar, even if it is keeping you from the life you ultimately want?

I know how uncomfortable and even downright painful it can be at times when you realize your standards have not been exactly what you'd like.

But it doesn't have to be. This is where we get to connect and realign.

No judgment, just curiosity.

Isn't it interesting that even though I don't like how disrespectful this person is to me, I still keep hanging out with them? I wonder why. What am I afraid of happening if I stand up for myself?

Isn't it interesting how I started my plan to work out five days a week, but as soon as someone invites me to something else, I do that instead? What was my reason for working out in the first place? Is that more important than this movie or coffee date? Am I using this as an escape instead of showing up for myself?

I have clean meals made up in the fridge, yet I still stopped and spent money on fast food on the way home. I wonder what I was trying to disconnect from or numb?

When we get curious, we are holding all of our parts accountable to a certain standard. We all know when something doesn't feel right. We all have that gut intuition. Even if it's been quieted down after so many years of being ignored, it's there.

Your intuition knows what is best for you, even if you don't trust it yet.

It takes time to build trust in yourself, but when you have the right system, the right support and the right accountability, it can happen with just a few steps.

Chapter Twenty-Six

TRUST YOURSELF

It still blows me away how the lack of trust in yourself can directly impact the choices you make and the chances you are willing to take.

I started with a new client last month who has been a clean and sober member of an Anonymous program for over thirty years.

Everyone in the program looked up to her, and with so much time under her belt, she felt that she should have all the answers. But she didn't. In fact, she was losing more and more faith in herself as the years went on.

She suffered from severe codependency and the constant service requirements of the twelve-step program only fueled the fire.

She felt like she was completely torn between what she wanted and what they expected of her.

We hadn't even finished the first session when I could see relief flood her entire being.

"What do you want?" I asked her.

It was a simple question, but I could see how caught off guard she was by it. It had been a lifetime since someone had actually asked her that.

In all her years of service, she had never felt that she was worthy of going after her own dreams full force. She was too consumed by the threat of relapse if she didn't do absolutely everything that was asked of her. But when she finally broke through what she was supposed to want into what she really wanted, it all came flooding out.

"I want time for myself. I want to say 'no' sometimes. I want to start my own business. I want to have a life I look forward to living."

I let her sit and feel into her wants and desires for a moment before I let her in on a little secret: "You are allowed to create any life you want. You don't need anyone's permission."

The look on her face was priceless—like a child being told they could have anything they wanted for Christmas.

Skepticism filled the space at first, but I could see her eyes light up with potential and her shoulders relax as if a weight she'd been carrying all these years had finally fallen off.

I could see her body shift forward in anticipation. Doubtful, but curious.

I had triggered a knowing inside of her that she'd been shutting out for decades. Deep down, she knew the truth; I just had to remind her.

We are the only ones who can decide what is true for us in our lives. Most of us were never meant to fit into any boxes or molds. We were meant to be different. We were meant to lead our *own* movement. Meant to challenge the status quo.

Sometimes we're told we're too loud or take up too much space.

Sometimes we're told we are broken and don't have what it takes.

Sometimes we're told who we are supposed to be, but that is not who we are.

But *that*, my friend, is for you and *only you* to decide.

Service is and always will be a huge part of who she is. A part of both of us, really. By encouraging her not to say 'yes' to every commitment, I am in no way asking her to stop being of service. I am asking her to consider her own needs as important as everyone else's, so that she can create a sustainable life and career of serving others.

The fact is, we need her and everyone like her who is trying to make a difference in this world to be able to do it for as long as possible. That won't happen if she burns herself out.

Taking our own needs into consideration is a step towards taking accountability for ourselves and our own life.

When we pay attention to what we need and honor ourselves by actually taking care of our health, happiness, and wellbeing, we develop a deep sense of trust and belonging within us. We stop doubting our worth or placing our value on how much we do for others. Instead, we take care of ourselves, and as a result, we are much better at being there for the ones we love and wish to serve.

The End

Ha! Just kidding. But if I had ended there, would you have been looking for some direction? Have you signed into the book portal yet? If you have, then you know this is absolutely just the beginning. If you haven't, what's stopping you?

There are tons of ways for us to connect and for you to begin your personal journey to lifestyle recovery.

The Freedom Framework is a simple strategy, but limitless in the ways it can set you free.

People-pleasing, procrastinations, perfectionism, disconnection, unhealthy habits, insecurities, self-doubt, powerlessness over your circumstances are all choices. Once you not only realize why you are making those choices, but then decide to change them, all you need is support to hold yourself accountable.

You are meant to experience joy and personal freedom. You're meant to experience all the amazing things that this life has to offer.

You are worth the time, energy, and investment.

I promise.

XO
Jenn

ABOUT THE AUTHOR

Jenn Henry is a well respected certified life coach specializing in lifestyle recovery and is dedicated to assisting individuals in prioritizing their own mental, emotional and physical well-being. With an unwavering passion for personal growth, mental health advocacy, and holistic wellness, Jenn has committed her professional journey to empowering others to take charge of their own futures.

As the founder of Lifestyle Recovery Solutions, and having battled her own challenges with mental health, addiction and codependency, Jenn provides comprehensive resources and unconditional support to individuals seeking recovery from people pleasing and codependency, overwhelm, lifestyle addictions, trauma, and mental health challenges such as anxiety and chronic burnout.

Jenn Henry's authentic dedication to helping others, coupled with her extensive expertise in the field of holistic lifestyle recovery, continues to positively influence countless lives. To learn more about Jenn Henry and her invaluable work, scan the QR code for access to the Resilience Book Portal.

Made in the USA
Las Vegas, NV
19 August 2023

76302378R00095